Right Girl, Wrong Box

Andrea Brasier

Trilogy Christian Publishers
A Wholly Owned Subsidiary of Trinity Broadcasting Network
2442 Michelle Drive
Tustin, CA 92780

Cover design by: Cornerstone Creative Solutions

For information, address Trilogy Christian Publishing
Rights Department, 2442 Michelle Drive, Tustin, Ca 92780.
Trilogy Christian Publishing/ TBN and colophon are trademarks of Trinity Broadcasting Network.

For information about special discounts for bulk purchases, please contact Trilogy Christian Publishing.

Manufactured in the United States of America

10 9 8 7 6 5 4 3 2 1

Library of Congress Cataloging-in-Publication Data is available.

ISBN 978-1-63769-040-6 (Print Book)
ISBN 978-1-63769-041-3 (ebook)

Dedication

To Jesus: You helped these ideas flow like crazy,
and I couldn't put my pen down while writing!
To my Mom and Dad: You've always been
an ever-present encouragement!
To the ladies at FCFC in Clovis, New Mexico: Thank God
for your words of wisdom, counsel, and weekly hugs!
To my dear friends Marvenar, Brenda, and Jess: Thank
you so much for loving me and being there for me.
To my husband, Joe: We have been through
so much! Thank you for standing by me.

Acknowledgments

Thank you, Holy Spirit, for being in me, speaking to me, and leading me. You persistently love me and bring me through things that I still don't understand at times. Lots of times. You've never left me.

Contents

Introduction: An Honest Beginning.....................................1

The Tissue Box...7
The Toy Box..17
Box of Chocolates 25
Hatbox..33
Matchbox...45
Ring Box...55
The Empty Box..63
The Gift Box...73
Coupon Box..85
The Crayon Box..91
The Black Box...101
The Shoebox 111
The Toolbox..121
Jack-in-the-Box 133
Box of Bones 139

Introduction

An Honest Beginning

I've honestly been putting off beginning to write this book. I've got a million ideas floating around, and aside from jotting down a few, I've been avoiding capturing those fleeting thoughts and putting pen to paper. The truth is, I'm afraid to disappoint, to put you off as the reader, or put off God with my ramblings. Deep inside, I feel that I am not enough for this task. Thoughts come and go but get wrestled back into submission. Do I have anything worth saying? I'm thirty-six, almost thirty-seven, but who's counting? I'm a mom of three sons. I'm a housewife. I'm an artist and a budding writer. I love coffee, Jesus, and exercise. Yes, I said I like to exercise! I love my golden retriever. Did I mention that I love coffee? What kind of sane mom wouldn't? I'm married to a military man who is currently deployed. I live clear across the country from any family and have to be Wonder Woman every single day!

My days are busy, to say the least. They are stressful, joyful, and mundane at times. They become monotonous very often. Can we say Groundhog Day? I love singing to Jesus at the top of my lungs in my backyard at night, either in my rocking chair or in my hammock. Oh yes, I have a

1

hammock, and I sing in it! If you are my neighbor, I'm sure I am loud at times, but hey, free concert, anyone?

I have to hold it all together because this is how my life is at the moment. Sometimes I really do forget that I am not alone. I forget that in this microcosm of mine that I have Jesus always with me. I'm not meant to battle this life all alone.

As a matter of fact, there is a sign above my coffee maker saying so. The battle is not yours, but God's. I get so worked up every day trying to be and do it all. I'm trying to be everything to everyone and hold this fort of mine together under these labels I've slapped onto myself, as well as ones put on me by others. This got me thinking about boxes. Boxes? Yup, boxes. My life in boxes! Either I, myself, or other people and events have put me in them for my entire existence, but I am so tired of being defined by them. The temptation to do so is beyond easy, but it is such a mess to undo.

Imagine your life in a closet, a massive walk-in closet. You open the door to see what you've stashed away. You started with one box, but soon you've accumulated an entire room full. They are stacked floor to ceiling. Small, large, gigantic, minuscule, you name it. Some are old. Some are new. Some are tattered and moth-eaten, while others are pristine and untouched.

You step into the closet that had evolved from a three-shelf hole-in-the-wall storage room to a massive ensuite, a private dressing room. Your day has begun, and you select the mood for the day. But what box will you choose? Your eyes roam over them. They not only cover the floor to ceiling but wall to wall. You take a tentative breath and put forth one bare toe into that space. Your fingertips twitch, almost ache, in anticipation over which box to select, trailing over lids, some clean, some laden with dust. You quickly avoid the old dusty ones because unpleasant feelings arise in you at contact: memories of what you shoved away in those boxes surface. You'll leave them for another day.

Your feet glide across the carpet until you stop in front of what you believe will be perfect for the day. This glass box shows off beauty, former glory, good memories, a bit of intrigue: you get the picture. As you reach for it, you realize it is stuck. You gently tug and wiggle the sides of the box, but smudges appear on the glass surface as you do. You furrow your brow. You get more and more frustrated as you shimmy the sides free. You huff in frustration in the silence of the closet. Eventually, the glass box slides free from the stack that sheltered it, but you hear a low-lying rumble. The towers of boxes surrounding you begin to shake. They start to fall from the top, and there is nothing you can do. You don't want to drop the beauty in your hands, but the room is about to cave in on you. In a last-ditch effort at self-preservation, you turn to run, glass box in hand. You almost escape, but down come the boxes. And down you go. The glass box shoots out of your hands and shatters just beyond the closet door.

All of your precious boxes have piled on top of you. Lids are jumbled, contents spilled, and there you are. A balled-up mess of woman, curled up on the floor, covered in things that you've saved, hidden, treasured, and forgotten. You're a mess, a hot mess, all because of a box. In your heart, you are hurt, as well as your backside. I'm sure your bottom hit the ground hard in the attempt to outrun that avalanche. Your mind is whirring, wheels turning over how ungraceful your fall was in the attempt to save your precious box. Your hair is all over your face. You haven't bruised anything, but your pride sure is taking on some nasty discoloration.

You blow your hair out of your eyes in a very unladylike fashion as you push yourself up to sitting. Mounds of boxes surround you. What a debacle! Memories are spilling out, some good, some bad. Some frighten the daylights out of you. You remember your precious glass box again, and your smile turns into a massive frown. The shattered pieces and the box's contents lay just beyond your reach. You don't want to, but you decide on another box for the day. Which one should you pick? Nothing seems to be able to replace the one that you lost.

What if you didn't have to choose? What if the boxes didn't even matter? What if all of the stuff that fills these boxes isn't worth a dime? Not a single dime! All of the labels, the contents, the secrets: just garbage. Would that rock your world? No more boxes to choose from or mood to set? No opinions to live up to or secrets to hide? Everything could be out in the open. I bet the audacity of that image makes your skin crawl.

How about this. You don't need a single box because what you have is broken and no good to anyone else. You could return each one to the manufacturer and get a refund. Would you do it? Would you exchange your brokenness with the only one to whom it matters for something priceless? I know I would! Without a doubt! Relinquishing your treasures and secrets can be hard. Scratch that, it seems nearly impossible! Maybe these boxes are broken, but they belong to you. Can I tell you something? The stuff you're clinging to? It isn't worth it.

This life, whether you love or hate it, isn't about the stuff. Why not let go of all of that stuff hindering you? Give it all over to the only person that can make you whole. Give it all over to your Maker. He is a gentleman and will take your broken pieces ever so tenderly. I'm in this mess with you. We stand side by side. You are never alone. We are all walking together in this life, changing from glory to glory.

We are slowly being perfected as we hand over our boxes. One at a time. Piece by piece. We are all fractured. So, let's be rid of our junk. Can I get an amen? Here's to the first box being returned! Huzzah! Yup, I totally said huzzah! You can return that box, and you don't even need a receipt!

The Tissue Box

Pleasant thoughts probably come to mind when you think of this innocuous little box. It comes in sweet packaging, promising to remedy your current ailments. Your box of tissues could be covered with flowers, cartoons, superheroes, or hearts. Regardless of what is on the outside, the tissues stand ready to aid you in the battle of cleaning something up and quickly disposing of them. Usually, this entails someone's running nose, boogers, blood, or even tears in response to an emotional meltdown, a cheesy feel-good movie, or even a random nosebleed from dry air.

The box has been packaged with a plan to come to your aid whenever and wherever you should choose to use them. Sure, you can choose by the pattern on the outside, the tissue count, or if your fluffy tissues are dry or full of soothing aloe for your possibly red and chafed nose, but that's about it. You've allowed someone somewhere to make decisions for you on how you're visually stimulated and physically soothed.

Okay, so maybe tissue box purveyors are not necessarily evil masterminds, plotting your demise based on market research and your biological probability to become ill so they can infiltrate your home, but the idea is fascinating in regards to your life. What kind of person, activity, or thing have you permitted to gain access to your life with the promise of physical and emotional healing? You believe you've chosen whatever that is or was and that you're in control of it all. No worries. You've got this!

In reality, your idea of comfort and healing was selected for you by someone or something that didn't even know you but begged to be part of your life and to provide you with a false sense of security. Let's say it is or was a person. You meet someone that looks so good on the outside. Everything about them is appealing. They wear the trendiest clothes. They smell like heaven. Their words pour over your soul like sweet honey, filling up every crevice of your aching heart. This person is a proverbial knight in shining armor on a white stallion. You let your aches and pains have a voice and pour out your heart: The bad, the ugly, and the shameful. This knight of yours pulls you gently to his chest and from nowhere procures a pristine handkerchief while your words turn into guttural sobs. That's right, girls, this fella has an actual, honest to goodness, handkerchief!

He hands it to you while simultaneously caressing your hair with his other hand. Your cries begin to subside as you daintily dab at your eyes with Sir Charming's hankie. Perhaps you throw in an unladylike nose-blowing session. His hand ceases to stroke your locks of messed up hair, and you sheepishly look up into his face. Hopefully, he will find you to be absolutely adorable with your puffy eyes and reddening nose.

Maybe now that your crying is over and the snot is all blown out, he will kiss you. How charming! You raise your pensive face to his gorgeously stunning one and begin to pucker and lean in for a kiss. After all, the man came to your rescue after a very unrefined meltdown. It stands to reason that he deserves a reward from his lady fair, his damsel in distress.

He leans in closer, and you almost seal the deal with a sweet kiss when in the reflection of his shiny armor, you see another woman. She is in a predicament. Heck, it seems even worse off than your issues. Sir Charming hesitates when he feels your intended kiss grind to a halt. You look like a deer caught in the headlights, staring at his armor. He looks down at where your eyes have become glued. At once, your knight sees what you've been gawking at, and his once romantic embrace loosens its grip. His focus retrains on a new target.

You are released from his once loving and healing grasp and are left clutching the once immaculate handkerchief to your chest in confusion. This man, this hero, this rescuer, now pulls out yet another handkerchief from his person as he strides toward another woman to aid in her time of need.

Oh no, he didn't! What the heck just happened? How many of those things does he keep hidden in his armor? Sir Charming, my rear end! This man had, only moments before captivated your heart, listened to your current tragedies, relieved you of your tears and other leakages, and even almost painted what, in your mind, would have been a kiss of generous Rhett Butler proportions on you. And then he up and left.

You stand slack-jawed as you watch this guy go through the same motions with another woman. Girl, you're still holding the man's hankie! It is all sodden with your tears and snot, but you still have it. Do you feel any better as you watch him progress from not only this woman but to another? In your mind, he was a rescuer, a healer, and a lover of your soul. You believe you chose him, but he chose you in your frailty. You had him in your arms, ready to use for your convenience, but you're the one that got used. He was not what you thought he was. Lord have mercy, not one bit!

Want to know what the crazy thing about this is? Just like the tissues in the tissue box, filled with promises of comfort and healing, he wasn't your first attempt at healing, and he won't be the last. This is especially true if you bought a multipack of tissue boxes. You'll run through them, people, like disposable tissues, fully aware of the outcome, the need to be satiated in your discomfort, but never finding the right fit.

Can I let you in on a secret? Not one person or tissue in this world can fill that role and responsibility of healer and comforter. Not one. Oh, you can try. By all means, go ahead. You will only come up empty-handed, needing another box of tissues for your brand-new issues. Here is an extreme case of a need for healing and stubbornness because of the source found in 2 Kings 5:1–13.

> Now Naaman was a commander of the
> army of the king of Aram. He was a great
> man in the sight of his master and highly
> regarded because through him the Lord
> had been given victory to Aram. He was
> a valiant soldier, but he had leprosy.
>
> 2 Kings 5:1

Do you think having a nasty cold in the face of Sir Charming was bad? Imagine being ready to plant one on your knight, but your lips are partially eaten off, and your nose is in a state of decay. Sorry sister, but no tissue in the world will heal that mess.

Naaman was reported to be a handsome man, as well as having prowess in battle, so this leprosy was no doubt a blow to his pride and self-esteem. Raiders from his country had taken a girl captive from Israel, and she served Naaman's wife. This young lady took the liberty to speak to her mistress on Naaman's behalf to suggest that he see the prophet of God in Samaria to cure him of his leprosy.

The man actually took the servant girl's advice to go to Israel. He requested permission from his king to go and took so much money it would blow your mind. His king sent a letter to the king of Israel along with Naaman, requesting his healing. Now hold up a moment. Pause. Wasn't Naaman supposed to seek the Prophet in Israel? Not the king? Wrong tissue! The king of Israel received the letter and tore his robes at the audacity of it. He said he was not God and was Naaman trying to pick a fight with him?

Luckily, the message was heard, by Elisha, the man of God. He requested that Naaman come to him. Naaman pulls in, with full pomp and circumstance, horses and chariots, in front of Elisha's house. The prophet tells Naaman to wash in the Jordan River seven times, and he would be cleansed of leprosy. If that were me and my flesh was wasting away, I'd be doing cannonballs into that river. I'd rise out majestically and healed, perhaps singing like a light from heaven had appeared and shone on me in my shining moment.

This fella went away angry, fussing because the Jordan wasn't as clean as other rivers. Face...palm. Really? It looks like leprosy wasn't the only thing Naaman needed to be healed of. But I digress. Eventually, with some convincing, Naaman made his way back and down to the Jordan. Lo and behold, he came up cleansed with his handsome flesh restored and clean, like that of a young boy. Then he went back to Elisha, the man of God, and declared that he knew now that there was only one true God in the world, the God of Israel.

Why on earth would he put off something so simple for his healing? Because of pride? To save face? Because of doubt? This man didn't serve the God of Israel. He acted on his own beliefs, or lack thereof, and searched out healing but didn't go to the one who could heal him and make him whole. Isn't that like us. When we are sick or hurt, we reach for the tissues. We grab the box and run through them rampantly until the box is empty! We then grab another box. We sniffle, sneeze, cry, and we try to self-medicate. We exhaust all options because we've chosen the tissue box in hopes of self-medicating instead of calling on our Lord, the only one that can truly heal.

So, go on ahead and use up your tissues. Blow your nose until it is chafed and chapped. Binge-watch your favorite series online for that temporary fix. Or, you can come before the one and only Jehovah Rapha, the God who heals and let Him mend you.

I'd like to say many, if not most of you, have heard of the woman with the issue of blood. But, to be on the safe side, I'd like to introduce you to her. You can find her story in the book of Mark in the New Testament (Mark 5:22-34).

Jesus was on his way through the streets when he was approached by a synagogue leader named Jairus. This man fell at the feet of Jesus and pleaded for him to come heal his twelve-year-old daughter so that she wouldn't die. Jesus went with Jairus, and a large crowd followed. In the midst of all this, a woman who had been bleeding for twelve years showed up. She'd suffered immensely under the care of many doctors trying to find a cure. She spent all of her money in the process but instead of getting better with the deluge of remedies no doubt prescribed, she only got worse. She had heard about Jesus, and as a last-ditch effort, she made her way to the crowd in hopes of getting close enough to him. With just a touch of his garments, she believed she would be healed.

Was she successful? Yes! She was able to touch the hem of his garment, and immediately the bleeding stopped. She could feel it in her body! When Jesus felt power leave his body, he turned to the crowd and asked who had touched him. His disciples flat out mocked him over what they considered a foolish question since they were obviously in a large crowd, and everyone was bumping elbows with each other. This didn't deter Jesus from seeking out the person who had touched him. The woman knew she was healed, and in a moment of bravery, she fell at his feet, scared out of her mind, and admitted what she'd done.

In that time, women were to stay away from other people when they experienced their time of the month. They were considered unclean. And for her to come out into public while bleeding, and touch a man, a rabbi no less, well, that took a lot of bravery a whole lot of gumption, many would say foolishness, but she knew she had exhausted every other option to heal herself. She'd run through her tissue boxes to no avail. This time she was desperate because this disease was killing her. I can only imagine her on her knees, trembling, fearing what others would say, how she'd be castigated, cast out, perhaps spat on. Then Jesus spoke up.

He called her daughter! Then he told her that her faith had made her well and to go in peace, free from her suffering. Her heart was probably pounding out of her chest. She most likely worried that the crowd could hear it. I imagine this formerly ill woman stood on trembling legs and felt freedom for the first time in years. She was no longer held captive by this crippling illness. She wasn't required to stay hidden and be labeled unclean any longer. If I were her, I would have hugged Jesus, kissed his cheek, and said thank you. Then, I would have hiked up my robe and taken off down the streets shouting that I was healed! Jesus would have chuckled and grinned ear to ear as I cast a jubilant glance over my shoulder at him. Life would begin again! No more dang tissue box for me!

I can relate to this story so very well! I mentioned at the beginning of this book that my husband is in the military. We've moved our fair share, and God willing, we'll get orders soon to move again. Our previous base was in Germany. I was lucky enough, no, blessed enough to get a weekend away to a women's conference with ladies from my church. I'd had a tooth removed before going, so that was fun. On the way home, we stopped off to eat. It was my time of the month, but I noticed something wrong during a trip to the ladies' room.

Warning, you may be grossed out. I should have been finishing my period, but I began passing golf-ball-sized blood clots. Disgusting, right? It was also a bit frightening. I let my carpool buddy know, and we chalked it up to a heavy cycle, but the problem didn't stop there. Although I'd been surrounded by women from the church, I didn't think to ask for prayer. I continued bleeding for six weeks. Let me tell you how much fun that wasn't. Enter the self-treatment and reaching for the tissue box. I worried. I was afraid. I called my doctor. I begged to be seen by someone, anyone. I don't remember praying over the situation. I got an appointment and had a pelvic exam, including the dreaded pap smear.

They found a three-centimeter mass in my cervix that wouldn't budge. They tried to make it, but it wouldn't release its grasp. Right then and there, I began panicking. My grandma on my mom's side had passed away from ovarian cancer, so I was genetically a target. The hospital scheduled me for surgery to remove the invader and prescribed me a double dose of birth control pills to stop the bleeding, iron pills to prevent anemia, and stool softeners to help with the blockage issues from the iron pills.

I went home scared and angry, thinking I would die soon and leave behind my three sons and husband. I cried at our Wednesday night life group when I told our friends what was going on. After that, I became stubborn. I began to pray. I took my meds daily, and I prayed hard. I have been healed before by God, physically, and I prayed He would do it again. I brought up to God the woman with the issue of blood. I asked Him to heal me as he had healed her. I asked Him to do it, not only for my sake but for the nurses I would see at my pre-op appointment the day before the surgery. That day finally came, and I stayed in faith that God had healed me. I showed up, and they briefed me about the procedures for the next day. Yes, I said *briefed*. I'm a military spouse. We just get used to the lingo. Before my appointment ended, I asked if they could examine me again for the mass. I mentioned I had been praying for healing and didn't want surgery if I didn't need it. The nurse agreed and proceeded to examine me. She looked puzzled and excused herself for a moment only to return with another medical professional. She then told me it must have been one heck of a prayer because the mass was gone.

She was sure it would be there, smaller because of the meds, but still there. When all was said and done, I dressed and got ready to leave. I did not need surgery. The nurse said it would most likely reoccur, but I just smiled, thanked them, and told them that I would not be back! I walked out of that hospital feeling so relieved and free. No tissues needed for this girl! I may not have cried out to God in the beginning, but I got my bearings straight. He is Jehovah Rapha, God, my healer! He is the only true physician. He healed me, he boosted my faith, and Lord only knows what fire he lit in the nurses that attended me that day.

Now, I want to make something abundantly clear. God could have chosen not to heal me this side of heaven. I could have relied on my own methods of healing or crying out to

Him, or He could have taken me home to Jesus, where I would have been made whole from head to toe. Regardless of the possible outcomes, I realized that Jesus was and is the only one that could and can heal me. Girl, I'm not sure where you find yourself at this moment, but I urge you to go to Jesus first. Put that tissue box up and call your healer. He loves you so very much. Heck, He died for you! You can live for Him!

The Toy Box

As a little girl, I had the best toy box ever! My grandpa built it for my sisters and me. It had two little cubbies up top and a deep box underneath at a slant, with two sliding doors. This particular toy box allowed me while I was little to climb inside and hide from either my sisters or my parents. It was not a super comfy hiding place when filled with my toys but so worth the prime hiding spot! Who am I kidding? My toy box was never full because I thoroughly enjoyed allowing my toys the freedom to enjoy the parameters of my bedroom. I hated to clean up. Nothing has changed in a few decades of life in that respect. I still hate cleaning up. I hate cleaning up my toys, aka my art supplies. They, too, like their freedom!

Toy boxes have one purpose: to store the fun things in life until you choose to let them out to play. They represent a controlled anticipation of sorts. You purchase toys to have fun with them. You express your ideas through them as a vehicle for your hidden desires, frustration, life aspirations, and so much more. When the day is done, you pick up these toys and shove them back inside your toy box, ready for the next playdate or imagination session. You choose when, where, and how you play. You choose who you become in the presence of your friends or in the privacy of playing alone. When all is said and done, you either put the toys away with satisfaction for an adventurous mission well carried out or in shame because the only time you can be your true self is when you're pretending with an audience or by yourself.

As a little girl, I had a variety of toys I played with define the many facets of my personality. I played with Legos, baby dolls, toy swords, pop guns, stuffed animals, pretty plastic ponies, army men, tea sets, and much more. So many parts of my personality came out to play depending on the toy I chose or was given. Was I playing dolls with the dream house? I wanted to be the princess! All glitzy in peaches and cream, dressed in sequins. Building with Legos or wooden blocks usually turned into replicating small dream houses, bridges, and car garages, including even universal remotes. A girl can dream! I built, I played, I pretended, I imagined, and I longed for the worlds I was creating to be true even for a day.

I could be a hero on a mission one moment and Cinderella leaving the ball the next, praying my prince would chase me down to profess his undying love. We'd move into his castle where I could live out eternal bliss, dripping in jewels but also still be available to carry out secret and very stealthy rescue missions at night. This girl has goals!

But then the fantasy would end. My mom would have me pick up my room, toys included. The fantasies would be put away in the darkness of my toy box, and I would yearn after our next adventure. I'd ache for the chance to express my hidden desires because, on the outside, I just didn't feel comfortable enough in my own skin. I felt trapped and defined by my different interests and expectations of who I should be. Who was I? I was a princess who loved to play in the mud, draw and paint, climb trees, play dress up, wrestle, wear pretend jewelry, and more.

In retrospect, I learned to be ashamed of the different parts of me because I didn't believe I fit in anywhere in particular. I felt uncomfortable as a girl sometimes. I'm not sure why. The devil definitely went after my identity as a whole at an early age, trying to make me feel uncomfortable in my own skin. Like the many identities we take on when we play with our toys, we can easily allow them to define who we are based on lies of the devil being whispered into our ears either directly or through friends, family, and even strangers.

God loves when we use our imaginations. He gave them to us. I believe it is our job, along with the Holy Spirit, to align our dreams with the heart of God. We select these toys to play with at a young age, and what we played out can mold and shape us. God knows our hearts. He made them. As hard as it is to hear, but because He loves us, God will allow us to choose a toy and play out our desires, even when he knows they won't be good for us. He knows us and wants us to love Him freely. So, He lets us go. He allows us to choose those toys. His love is better than any falsity we would choose for ourselves, and hopefully, we will see the imperfections in our choices and allow them to refine us, and again seek God, what is holy, and what is good for us.

Perhaps it is cliché to bring up the prodigal son, found in Luke 15:11-31, but that story pegs the toy box message. Jesus began speaking a parable in Luke 15. Jesus continued: "There was a man who had two sons. The younger one said to his father, 'Father, give me my share of the estate.' So, he divided the property between them" (Luke 15:11–12). Now, hold on a minute!

This man-child had the audacity to ask for his inheritance, his toys, before his father was even dead. His father was not even sick. How rude! In the culture of the time, he was basically saying he wished his father was in the grave so he could have his goodies. His dad obliged and evenly divided his property between them. He divided his toys amongst his children. The younger son got together all he had, and he set off for a distant country. He squandered every bit of money, every toy, on wild living.

Eventually, when he had nothing, the land where he'd gone to, to get away from home with his goodies, experienced a severe famine. The whole country was in need. He had to hire himself out to feed pigs. He got so desperate for food that he even dreamed about eating the pigs' food. His people weren't allowed to consume pork. I can only imagine what a blow it was to his ego to want to share the food of something considered unclean.

He'd chosen toys he was not ready for. He wasn't grown enough to ask for what he asked from his father, but he did it anyway. He took what belonged to his father and flagrantly abused and flaunted and eventually lost his inheritance. All of this was in pursuit of being someone he was never meant to be. He took things from his father and tried to define himself outside of his dad's presence. He used his toys to play out a life that clearly was fake. His arrogance and pride and determination to live out a life unworthy of who he truly was, landed him in a foreign country, starving, broke, and stripped bare before strangers.

The beautiful thing about this story is that this younger son realized how destitute he was and made a plan to return home to his family. To his father, the one he basically wished dead for selfish reasons. I imagine he felt humiliated and scared to death to have to tuck his tail and head home to what he assumed would be a very cold welcome. Maybe his father would reject him. Maybe his dad would harbor bitterness for his wild child, turned reprobate. The younger son was so desperate that he risked ridicule and a possible shunning to go home and beg for work because he felt unworthy. When he approached, his father saw him while he was still far off.

Instead of turning his back on his son, he was filled with compassion and took off running toward him. He threw his arms around him and kissed him.

Can you imagine how shocked the boy was upon impact? He was probably winded, bewildered, and perhaps ready to cry. He even spouted out, maybe sputtered out, that he'd sinned against heaven and his dad and that he was no longer worthy of being called his son. Can you picture a young adult man crying in the presence of his dad, just begging for forgiveness for all he'd done? Meanwhile, his dad clutches his son by the face that is probably rough and unshaven and smiles through tears of happiness because his child that he'd assumed was dead was not only alive but back home with him and with a changed heart. He probably had to shake his son gently out of a stupor to focus on him so he could see and hear the truth of his welcome homecoming.

This beautiful man called for the best robe to be brought and put on his son. He also commanded a ring and sandals be placed on his son. The boy probably had snot flying by then as well as tears of joy blinding him. These items alone were probably enough to stun this young man, but more blessings came to celebrate his homecoming. The fattened calf was brought and killed to have a feast and celebrate! The father was ecstatic to have his boy back, regardless of what he'd done. His son, who was dead to him, was now back and alive. This young son was once again in the presence of his father. He was presented with gifts, toys, to identify who he was. It is such a beautiful image to see a father defining his son as his own, despite his faults.

As awe-inspiring as this was, there was another son in the picture, and he was raging with jealousy. This older son had been working in the field when he heard music and dancing. The ruckus intrigued him, so he inquired of a servant as to the meaning of it all. The reply stunned him. It enraged him. He actually refused to join the party out of bitterness. His father went out to him and pleaded with him to join the party. Instead of softening his heart, the older son spewed venom. He raved on about how he'd slaved away all of these years for his father, not even disobeying him. Ever! And what did he get? Nothing! Not even a young goat to celebrate with his buddies.

Whoa! He sure went off his rocker toward his dad! That's a lot of pent-up anger he unloaded, and perhaps rightfully so. But here's the problem. The whole time his brother was gone, the older brother had access to his father. He had access to his dad's presence, his blessings, and his possessions, but he wasn't confident in who he was as his son to ask for anything! He had access to so many toys, and he chose to hold a grudge against his little brother, and he chose to live in denial of what his father so freely offered! This just blows my mind! I'm not sure what is worse. You have everything, waste it all, but come back home and to your senses, or you have it all. You slave for approval, but you won't accept what your father has freely given.

I know without a shadow of a doubt that I am guilty of both! Thank God he forgives. He redeems. He gives us gifts, toys. He watches us open and find joy in them or even abuse them. He watches the gifts left and abandoned as well. How his heart must ache, grieve even, to open what he gives us freely, accept it, and find our identity in him.

We all come with toys of our own. We have gifts, talents, and personalities. We have inquiring minds and tender hearts. We are beautiful creations of God's love, and he only wants the best for us. But isn't it funny, even though he's the one that creates the gifts within us, that it is up to us to give them freely back to him?

He won't demand them to be handed over, but he longs for the day that we surrender what we thought we could play with to define ourselves. Like the father of the prodigal son, He's waiting for us to return home so he can welcome us, replace the toys we had with ones that claim us as his children, and declare us, though we were once dead in ourselves, alive in Him.

Box of Chocolates

The thought alone of a box of chocolates makes me smile. In my mind, I can see the scene from Forrest Gump where Tom Hanks describes life this way due to receiving some very insightful advice from his momma. All humor aside, I get it! I totally do! When I think about a box of chocolates stashed away in my closet, the pleasure center of my brain does an all-out happy dance! I can just imagine sneaking into my closet and very quietly removing a red velvety box shelved somewhere high and hidden from the sight and reach of my husband and kids.

Today might have been a tough day, and I just want to treat myself. I plop myself within the cover of my closet and sit on the carpet with my back to the wall, bare toes curling in and out of the carpet fibers while I gently slide the lid off of that heavenly secret delight. On the inside of the lid, there would be an illustrated display of each tantalizing delicacy, labeled as to what they each contained. Some are caramel and cream-filled, others filled with chocolate and peanut butter. Another might be a cherry cordial or truffles filled with chocolate ganache. Oooooh, the choices! I'd sit there with the box in my lap, wide open, mind you, and I'd pause. Should I indulge myself? Just this once? One? Maybe two? There were twenty in the box, so what harm would it do? I worked out today. I deserve it. No, wait, I shouldn't do this. If I have one, then I won't be able to stop myself.

No one would know! I think they wouldn't. My husband might. He'd hug me and catch a whiff of chocolate on my breath, and then a grin would spread across his face because he would know he caught me. Then he'd ask where the chocolate was hiding. My kids' ears would perk up because they hunt sweets like a shark smells blood in the water. Then I would be tempted to lie. Yup, I'd be so tempted to lay on a thick lie about how I'm working out to stay healthy, and there is absolutely no way I would break my commitment to losing weight and getting stronger, just for a brief interlude with a piece of chocolate or six. I mean, gosh, who does he think I am? A quitter? Nah. I'm not a quitter.

I'd prove it to him right then and there. I'd show him weight loss progress photos of myself and perhaps show him how many pushups I could do. Phew. I'm not a quitter. You're a quitter, just saying. Chocolate is a thing of the past. I'd strut out of the room with my head held high and my shoulders back because I *am awesome*! That's what I am. I am A to the W to the E to the some!

Okay, so that scenario just blew up in my mind and ran off on a tangent. The point being, is that I'm still in a hypothetical situation in my hypothetical closet, staring at my hypothetical box of chocolates and lusting after them. Also, I'm worrying over betraying the dedication I made to myself to get healthier and entertaining how the heck I'd cover up my guilt.

Suddenly what looked, smelled, and most likely would have tasted so good turned to ashes in my mouth. Buzzkill. The sad thing is as I gained the confidence to deny my flesh, the crinkling sound of the paper covering the chocolates would again alert my senses. The white barrier of paper separating me from the sweets would slide over just a tad bit revealing the glistening domed top of a ganache stuffed truffle. The divine scent would waft through the air, reaching my nostrils with a flourish, and as if on cue, my salivary glands would create a mini pool of slobber in my mouth. At this time, I'd have a choice to make. I could have no part of this moment because I know its ramifications on my health journey. Maybe I could have one or two pieces, enjoy them thoroughly, and make a plan to walk more that day in addition to my regular workout schedule. Or, I could cave emotionally and binge. Then I would feel sick to my stomach and in my heart because I chose to give in to temptation and blew it. I just flat out *blew it*!

You might find this situation absolutely hilarious, or it might grieve you and hit way too close to home. It is all a matter of perspective. The cocoa plant in and of itself isn't actually all that bad. Cocoa powder derived from the beans is actually quite beneficial to one's health. It can reduce inflammation in the body, improve your mood, improve cholesterol, and so much more. However, when additional ingredients are added to the cocoa powder, that's where the trouble begins. When you remove yourself from your source of well-being and begin to tamper with added ingredients, you may find yourself traipsing off after an idol of your own making in hopes that it will satisfy your cravings deep down in your flesh.

It doesn't have to be a box of chocolates. It could be the pursuit of money, success, attention, flattery, cars, social status, clothes, anything really. The lusts of the flesh take over when we allow temptation to woo us into thinking it can fill the God-shaped hole in our hearts when it most certainly won't. No matter how many chocolates in that box you shove into your mouth, the ache will persist. Go ahead and try! So many people do, and so many people fail. In their misery, they assume they can try another scheme or plan. This might appear to work on the surface level. You could have the looks, the money, the spouse, the 2.5 kids, the house, business, whatever, and still be dissatisfied. The entire book of Hosea in the Bible perfectly illustrates this! Please, oh please, take the time to read it!

When I was mulling over what story to pull from for this chapter, I remembered the story of Hosea. I recalled I had read a novel at one point about the story of a man named Hosea who fell in love with a prostitute. He adored her, but she felt so unworthy and kept running away from him, and from their marriage, and back to the brothel to sell herself. Hosea loved her so much that, despite her actions, he kept going after her to bring her home. He even paid her masters, who she'd willingly sold herself to, to buy her back.

I assumed the story of Hosea was about this: a woman that sank into depravity, drawn by the lusts of her flesh: Doing what she knew was wrong because she didn't have any self-respect, who was chased down by a man so deeply in love with her that he would keep no record of wrongs. He would choose her, again and again. Even though he knew she would probably continue to be unfaithful to him, he'd sacrifice everything to redeem her.

So romantic! So heartbreaking. So inaccurate. Well, partially. Please, stop right now and read the entire book of Hosea. I promise your heart will do some major flip-flops as you confront how violently passionate God is. He desired to redeem Israel so she would return unblemished into his loving arms. This part of his character blows me away!

> When the Lord began to speak through
> Hosea, the Lord said to him, "Go, marry
> a promiscuous woman and have children
> with her, for like an adulterous wife this

land is guilty of unfaithfulness to the
Lord." So he married Gomer daughter
of Diablaim, and she conceived and bore
him a son.

Hosea 1:2–3

Hosea and his adulterous wife Gomer were an analogy
for God and Israel. They were the picture of God, the bridegroom, and Israel, His unfaithful bride. God demonstrated
by their children's names and their ramshackle relationship
what a disgrace Israel was for straying from His perfect love
and provision.

The actual story of the prophet Hosea and his wife
Gomer is short but the anguish in God's heart toward his
people's infidelity lasts much longer. After everything he'd
done for Israel, they decided to lust after other lovers that
would give them food and water, wool, linen, olive oil, and
drink. She, Israel, burned incense to Baal, the false god. She
covered her body with rings and jewelry and went after her
lovers, forgetting her husband. Israel cursed, lied, committed
murder, stole, and, with eyes wide open, walked into affairs.
She rejected knowledge, ignored the law of her God, and
replaced his glorious self with something disgraceful. God's
people consulted wooden idols, used diviner's rods, and more.

If you thought that was terrible, there's much more.
God's anger raged at them, and he pleaded with them not to
infect Judah or Ephraim with their wayward behaviors. He
even calls them a stubborn heifer. That's right! God called
them a stubborn heifer. The Israelites are stubborn, like a
heifer, how then, can the Lord pasture them like lambs in the
meadow?" (Hosea 4:16).

Because Israel lusted after and fulfilled her desires outside of God and rejected what was good, an enemy would

surely pursue her. God was heartbroken. He was fuming! He made threats against his bride that made the hairs on the back of my neck stand up. I had such a hard time reading these angry words from God because I never believed the God that is love could feel that way. Then I thought about how I'd feel if my husband decided to cheat on me. The imaginary scenarios flew through my mind and gripped my heart. Keying his truck and taking a wooden bat to the headlights and possibly his head didn't even seem to come close to feeling vindicated in his supposed act of infidelity. I want to say I'd be a strong Christian woman, who would immediately seek counsel, prayer, and offer forgiveness, but I would probably like to take him out at the knee caps with a bat. Horrible, but the truth. I wouldn't do that, but my heart wants to go there.

I'm learning how to pray more and let God handle his business. So my wild imagination and the fake infidelity might go more like me dropping to the ground onto my knees and my heart breaking into a million pieces while pouring out my pain to Jesus. Maybe a bit of both the crazy would occur. I'm only human. But God? He is not human. He is not a man that he would lie. When he makes a commitment, he keeps it! He says,

> Woe to them because they have strayed from me! Destruction to them, because they have rebelled against me! I long to redeem them but they speak falsely. They do not cry out to me from their hearts but wail from their beds. They slash themselves, appealing to their gods for grain and new wine, but they turn away from me. When I fed them, they were satisfied; When they were satisfied, they

became proud; then they forgot me. Like
a bear robbed of her cubs, I will attack
them, and rip them open; Like a lion I
will devour them—a wild animal will
tear them apart.

Hosea 7:13–14; 13:6, 8

Wow! Just *wow*! This is a side of God I never saw before.
I wrestled with this part of Him until I thought about how
I would feel if it happened to me. His bride, His beautiful
Israel, left her husband for cheap thrills that often resulted
in pain to attain pleasure when she already had a willing
bridegroom.

God instructs His prophet, Hosea, to go after his flighty
wife to demonstrate to His people how much He loves them,
despite their trespasses. "'Go, show your love to your wife
again, though she is loved by another man and is an adul-
teress. Love her as the Lord loves the Israelites, though they
turn to other gods and love the sacred raisin cakes'" (Hosea
3:1). Hosea did as God commanded. He was to get his wife
and buy her back to redeem her and their marriage. And like
Hosea, God chose to pursue His people.

His heart changed within Him, and his compassion
was aroused. He did not carry out his fierce anger, but he
called to them like a roaring lion protecting His own, and
they came to Him trembling because they knew not only
what they'd done to themselves but what they'd done to their
Maker's heart. God does not rail on them but settles them
into their homes. Forget the guilty pleasure of a hidden box
of chocolates. I want this! And God would welcome me back.
He'd call me out of my lusts and chase me down. He'd toss
out that chocolatey substitute for His person, and He'd welcome me back into His arms. No condemnation. No fear.

31

No finger-wagging declarations of my weaknesses, just love, peace, and wholeness. Home.

Girl, I encourage you whatever it is that you've tossed God aside for, even unwittingly, drop it. Let it go. Don't be defined by your chocolate box surrogate instead of by God. You aren't what you run after. You are not your job, wealth, hobbies, clothes, talents, looks, and how your family sees you. You cannot satisfy your cravings outside of God. Go to the ends of the earth or the depths of the ocean, but you won't be appeased.

> Jesus says, "I am the vine; you are the branches. If you remain in me, you will bear much fruit; apart from me you can do nothing. If you do not remain in me, you are like a branch that is thrown away and withers; such branches are picked up, thrown into the fire and burned. If you remain in me and my words remain in you, ask whatever you wish, and it will be done for you."
>
> John 15:5–7

God encourages us to remain in Him not only for our sake but because we are a living testimony to the world. Our lusts can cause the eyes of innocents to become blind. I'd rather stay close to the source of true life and be a light in this world, than to lead others into darkness.

I'm gonna leave the box of chocolates on the floor.

Hatbox

I never saw my grandma in any hat but one. She was a classy, sassy, and strong German woman. She made her way to the USA after marrying an American army man who would become my grandpa. My grandma's name was Ingebourg, Inge for short. She had the most beautiful black hair, tan skin, and warm brown eyes. She always had a smile and a strong hug for me. I used to rub her earlobes between my fingertips when I hugged her because they were so soft. She would just laugh and pat me with her firm hands while I hugged her, standing as she sat. She sat in the same spot at her table every day, not at the head, but one chair over to the side. That's a custom I have taken on. I have my chair, and no one is allowed to have it. That may sound a bit selfish, but it feels special and nostalgic to me.

My grandma learned English by watching American soap operas. She'd get so wound up and would shake her fists at the characters. That always made me laugh because I knew they weren't real people. I used to crawl onto her lap in the recliner and sit for a while until she'd tell me to stand up in German. "Steh Auf!" Because of her dialect, auf sounded more like oof. She also pronounced my name as it should be in German. To this day, peoples still mess up the pronunciation of my name, and I cringe.

My grandma could cook like no one you've ever met. She drank coffee and smoked cigarettes on the back patio along with my aunt while I swam in the pool with my sisters and cousins. She also had an upright piano that she could play. The woman taught herself to play because she grew up poor and couldn't afford lessons.

I remember her wearing a long dressing gown every day. Usually black or a deep purple with some embroidered design up along the neckline. Along with my sisters, I'd sneak peeks into old photo albums to see when my grandma was younger. She and my grandpa had parties and company over a lot then, and she dressed to impress. I would also go through her closets in the basement bedrooms. I was that kid, curious as anything! In addition to my grandpa's old army uniforms, she had some pretty snazzy outfits in there. There was this one dress that had slinky straps, and I loved it! It was iridescent black and gold and felt so magical! Somehow, I was able to bring it back home on one of my visits. We lived two hours away in Warner Robins, Georgia, while they lived in Lawrenceville.

I used to play dress up in that beautiful thing. I have pictures of my best friend and me all dolled up. I wore that dress and my mom's heels. Both were way too big for me, but I didn't care. She and I made pretend crowns and bracelets from some linking plastic blocks, and we sure flashed some silly grins for the camera! I loved that dress! It did not come with accessories. Like I mentioned before, I've only ever seen my grandma in one kind of hat. It did not come in a box with a fancy handle. It was not a vintage mint cream. It was made not of crushed velvet and precisely placed feathers that would tickle your ears as you strode elegantly through the room with every single eye on you.

This hat was not a red sequined affair, shimmering in the moonlight or even a raspberry beret. My grandmother was a sassy and classy lady, but her hat was not. No suede or lace trim bedecked her covering or rhinestones that would steal the show. It was nothing ostentatious, daring, or bold. Although it was new, she wore it only out of a desire to preserve her dignity in a time of despair. The hat she wore was a terry cloth turban, and she wore it like a queen, all smiles, even though on the inside she was dying. Ovarian cancer was attacking her body and required chemotherapy as a treatment, paired with steroids. The chemo took her beautiful black hair, and the steroids puffed up her face and her belly like she was six months pregnant.

I remember visiting her on the oncology floor, where my mom worked as a nurse. She smiled and held my hand while she gabbed on with me and my mom. She looked so dignified in that hat of hers. She never let on to her discomfort or showed embarrassment at having lost her hair or how the steroids were disfiguring her. That hat of hers offered her a covering from the illness that would ultimately take her life. It was a covering in a time of need. It created a conduit for the seen and the unseen. In my heart, I knew she was ill, but my mind shut it out based on what laid before my eyes: a semblance of normalcy.

I was sixteen when we laid her to rest. She had a small teddy bear clutched to her chest in her casket and a peaceful smile on her face: no more cancer and no more hat. I don't know if she believed in Jesus, but I pray that she did. I can imagine Him leading her into eternity by hand, healed, whole, and with a head full of glorious black hair. No more need for the covering of her old hat; she was under the covering of Jesus now. She was probably having a full conversation in German with Him too. Now that makes me smile!

I, myself, own quite a few hats, but only one that belongs in a protective case. I have several ball caps in a bathroom drawer for after I finish working out, errands, and in general bad hair days. Each one sports a state that I have lived in, Georgia being my favorite. They bring smiles to my face, and fun conversations seem to ensue with strangers that assume the college teams my hats advertise are of the utmost importance to me. I am not in the least bit interested in college or pro ball. Not one bit. They ask me what teams I root for. I just chuckle because I don't want to argue with them over who is the best, etc. I just like the hats. My only goal is to cover my dirty hair from my workout sweat fests.

The one I keep in a case is not technically a hat, but I treasure it above all others. I handle it with the utmost care, respect, and awe. It is the tiara that I wore on my wedding day. It is delicate, regal, and it glimmers in the light. I remember wearing it with my empire waist wedding dress with a sheer but floral embroidered back. Silk domed buttons traipsed up my back while my cathedral veil gracefully flowed down my back to the ground.

That tiara made the feel like royalty when I married my husband almost eleven years ago. I felt glorious in my entire ensemble and nauseated. I'm not gonna lie, the butterflies in my stomach must have morphed into ravenous, hunger-blocking, nerve-wracking, little boogers: more like a herd of ravenous raptors. We even had a chocolate fountain and fresh fruit to dip into it. My raptors kept me from enjoying more than a fourth of my meal. Forget the fountain. But, I had my tiara, and I looked good! I was under the covering of a bridal glow. I was now my beloved's, and my beloved was mine.

As beautiful as that moment was, as dazzling as I felt with those jewels I wore on my gorgeously coiffed hair, the covering my "hat" provided was only temporary. I went from daughter to wife in a matter of minutes, but neither title nor role defined me as a whole. Only one covering could offer that for me, and I can't find that in a hat. There is no permanent protection from the ravages of cancer in a rhinestone tiara, Georgia ball cap, or turban. Only the representation of protection.

At the beginning of time, God created the world and everything in it, including man and woman. He made light and separated it from the darkness, calling them night and day. He spoke, and the land and the seas appeared. He called forth vegetation: seed-bearing plants and trees. Again, he spoke, and in the creative explosion of his breath, out of his love for us, he created the sun, moon, and stars.

> And God said, "Let there be lights in the vault of the sky to separate the day from the night, and let them serve as signs to mark sacred times, and days and years and let them be lights in the vault of the sky to give light to the earth." And it was so. God made two great lights— the greater light to govern the day and the lesser light to govern the night. He also made the stars. God set them in the vault of the sky to give light on the earth, to govern the day and the night, and to separate the light from the darkness. And God saw that it was good. And there was evening, and there was morning—the fourth day.
>
> Genesis 1:14–19

Imagine that magnificent display of lights! The sheer majesty of it all brings me to tears. Newborn stars would shiver and shake with excitement as they burst forth with dazzling light for the very first time in the presence of their maker. I believe God stood by and marveled as he took in an aromatic breath from the freshly grown trees, mountains, and flowers. He'd beam with pride, and His pearlescent teeth would reflect the loving glow of the sun's light beaming from the moon. But he wasn't done yet, not even close! Next, he'd speak yet again, and the oceans, skies, and land would produce living creatures to roam freely and joyfully under the eye of their Maker.

As if that wasn't enough, God went further. He decided to make mankind. This was the first time as well that he referred to Himself as Us, the Holy Trinity. God the Father. God the Son. God the Holy Spirit.

> Then God said, "Let us make mankind in our image, in our likeness, so that they may rule over the fish in the sea and the birds in the sky, over the livestock and all the wild animals, and over all the creatures that move along the ground." So, God created mankind in his own image, in the image of God he created them; male and female he created them.
> Then the Lord God formed a man from the dust of the ground and breathed into his nostrils the breath of life, and the man became a living being
> Genesis 1:26–27; 2:7

I want you to pause and catch what you just read. Everything else was spoken into creation, but God in His majesty stooped down, probably kneeled in the dirt, and scooped up clay to make us by hand. Every muscle fiber, sinew, bone, strand of hair, color-filled iris, brain synapse, fingerprint, and more, God sculpted by hand. He worked until His masterpiece was almost perfect, but not complete. Adam's body remained lifeless on the ground in the presence of the Maker. That is, until God, Himself, breathed life into the entire human race through one human body.

I imagine Adam awoke with a gasping breath, filling up his newly formed lungs with air and breathing in the scent of the surrounding flora and fauna. His chest would rise and fall to the cadence of his rapid but steadily beating heart. Everything was new but familiar at the same time. There was a familiarity in his surroundings and a startling realization he wasn't alone or unknown.

His bare hands would dig into the dirt beneath him, the same dirt he was created from just moments before. The grit of it all would embed itself beneath his fingernails as his muscles fired for the first time, raising his body into a seated position. The heady rush that would come from his rapid change of position would make his pulse race as he finally made eye contact with his Creator.

Adam and God would smile deeply at each other. Created and Creator would have a deep knowing. "Hello, Adam," God would say. "Happy birthday! I've been so eager for you to finally meet me, even though I knew you before I made this world for you. This meeting has been a long time coming. Welcome home, son."

Adam's face would shine like the sun, basking in the glory and warmth of his Maker's words and very presence. A conversation would naturally flow as God stood and pulled Adam to his feet and gave him the grand tour of the wealth surrounding him and under his feet. Adam would gasp in delight as he and God would stand on a precipice and take in a panoramic view of the precious creation of the earth. God would then step back and watch the first of mankind as all living creatures would begin the steep incline to meet him to be named.

He must have chuckled as Adam fumbled awkwardly over the millions of vowels and consonants combining and flowing out of his mouth in rapid succession to declare the names over animals that were probably nuzzling his hair by now and sniffing his naked backside out of curiosity. Even after naming every living creature, God could tell it was not good for man to be alone. He noticed the fallen countenance of Adam's face as each male and female living being walked away in tandem with purpose and functionality. Ladies, this is where we came in.

> So the Lord God caused the man to fall into a deep sleep; and while he was sleeping, he took one of man's ribs and then closed up the place with flesh. Then the Lord God made a woman from the rib he had taken of the man, and he brought her to the man.
>
> Genesis 2:21-22

How shocked and in awe Adam must have been when Eve's beautifully delicate and feminine hand was transferred from God Almighty's into his very own. He probably stared endlessly into her velvety soft eyes as rivers of long dark hair cascaded over sensationally formed shoulders and whipped around them both tenderly in a breeze carrying dandelion seeds along with it.

For the second time, Adam met someone he'd never seen before, but somehow, he knew them so deeply, and intimately it made his heart want to burst, and tears threaten to pour over his cheeks. Eve must have felt the same way. Her Creator tenderly helped her stand as only a gentleman would and handed her over to a breathtakingly handsome man, as a father gives away a bride to her groom. "Adam and his wife were both naked, and they felt no shame" (Genesis 2:25).

God gave Adam and Eve dominion over the fish in the sea, the birds in the sky, and every living creature that moves on the ground. He blessed them and told them to be fruitful and multiply in number, filling and subduing creation. What a gift! This gift came with a garden and a covering, and with that covering came a decision to be made. Eden was so inviting that it captured the interest of a slithering, conniving, jaded, has-been perpetrator.

Satan, the devil, the former worship leader in heaven, who had his keister kicked out, was roaming upon the earth, looking to mess up the divine image of God through His people. God had offered the entire world to Adam and his bride. The whole world! He gave all of the plants bearing seeds and fruit to them as food. Even the tree of life would be under that umbrella, but there was one exception. The tree of the knowledge of good and evil was off-limits. It was lush and pleasing to the eye but would bring death to those who ate of its fruit.

I've never noticed that before. Adam and Eve could have chosen to eat from the tree of life. They would have been immortal and forever with God and perfect in every way. Imagine that, the ultimate enjoyment of peace, joy, and love with our divine Father. We'd have no pain, hatred, sickness, heartbreak, anxiety, suicide, depression, loneliness, starvation, greed, infidelity, divorce, death, or betrayal.

It baffles my mind. We had a covering, we had God's protection, and we had Him. We had everything we needed, but it wasn't enough. God didn't want robots obeying out of responsibility or specific designs as if under compulsion. God's heart ached to be in relationship with someone who freely chose Him, so he allowed us to choose. And we chose wrong.

The devil gambled and took a chance on our possible disobedience. He changed forms into the craftiest of creatures, the serpent, and slithered his way into the garden alongside Eve as she strode through the most magnificent orchard we'd ever see. She must have been hungry as she plodded along barefoot through the beautiful place her Lord had created for her. The sights and sounds would have tantalized enough, but she was also hungry. I'm sure that helped to sway her decision as the snake caught her off guard by speaking. No other animal had spoken to her before until this serpent engaged her in a full-fledged conversation in hopes of ruining what God had made pure and innocent.

The thing that blows my mind is that Eve was not alone. Her husband was present and nearby. Adam knew what God had commanded them to do. God said, do not eat of that tree. The devil distorted the words of the Almighty to corrupt creation and to soothe his embittered scaly self. If he couldn't be on top, then he didn't want to be.

Eve saw that the food was pleasing to the eye and good for food. So, she took it and ate it, then she handed it to her husband, and he ate it. And through one man, sin entered the world. Their eyes opened, and shame and fear crept in. They realized they were naked, so they hid.

I bet the devil watched from the shadows of the nearby plants, his forked tongue flicking in and out of his mouth. He radiated with satisfaction at having poisoned Adam and Eve with doubt, death, and sin, a special treat from the prince of darkness, a blackened, candy-coated piece of fruit, delicious to him and so full of leaching venom.

God's covering was gone. Adam and Eve died on the inside and came alive to sin. They sewed together fig leaves and made coverings for themselves. What was once perfect before, between them and God, became tainted. Even though God knew where they were, He still called to them, asking where they were and what they had done.

Lies, blaming, and curses became prevalent and shot infectious roots through the soil of the earth and into the hearts and minds of mankind. The Lord God made clothing out of the skins of animals for Adam and Eve in his kindness, but he had to banish them before they ate of the tree of life and gained immortality in their broken state.

From then on, the shedding of blood through animal sacrifices was necessary for a temporary covering until Jesus would come and reconcile us to God. He is the divine milliner making bespoke creations out of us. He knew us in our mother's womb. The hat He made us is a gift freely given. He carefully planned, crafted, and perfected His timing so He could present us with the only covering that would ever work.

How amazingly marvelous that God would choose to rescue us through the death and resurrection of Jesus Christ, the one and only covering for our sins that would penetrate, fill, and bathe our heart with His righteousness.

So, girls, drop these hats. Fling them into the air. Let them fall to the ground. Set them on fire if you must. Trade your ashes for the beauty of Christ's eternal covering. Raise those stunningly radiant crowned heads of yours and stand unashamed and protected in the presence of your Maker, the lover of your soul, the one and only Prince of Peace. "Therefore, there is now no condemnation for those who are in Christ Jesus, because through Christ Jesus the law of the Spirit who gives life has set you free from the law of sin and death" (Romans 8:1–2).

Matchbox

Have you ever been stuck between a rock and a hard place? I'd like to find the person who coined that phrase and clobber them over the head for reminding me of the messes I get in. And to profusely thank them for understanding and depicting the precise image of said difficult situations.

On February 17 of this year, I found myself in one of the most painful situations I've ever been in. My husband was three months into his deployment, and I was home with three kids to look after, and I was very sick.

My oldest son was not home that weekend but at a friend's house. I woke up that Friday with a very painful and hard lump in my neck, stemming from my eustachian tubes. The fever came and went. The flu was going around at the schools, taking out several students and teachers. On top of that, I am very allergic to where I live, so any little cold or flu bug could cause a severe sinus infection with retracted eardrums, fluid in my ears, vertigo, and burning in the bones and surrounding my eye sockets and the base of my skull.

I assumed it would be okay and go away with some home remedies and standing upright for the sinuses to drain, and with time. I was very wrong. The symptoms only got worse, and finally, two days later, I drove myself to the emergency room along with my two younger sons. My oldest son told me in a text message that it was not his problem and for me to deal with it. He would not come to my aid. I finally made it to the triage room, where I was checked for the flu by a lady forcefully shoving a long cotton swab into my already inflamed nasal cavity. I cried and continued crying when I was sent back to the waiting room. There I was with two young kids, abandoned by my oldest child, with my husband was across the world. The majority of the people in the waiting room had face masks on to prevent spreading the flu. Although surrounded, I felt very alone.

I was eventually called back and placed in a tiny waiting room no larger than a small bathroom. My husband contacted me through messages online. I cringed when I had to tell him why the boys were with me instead of home with their big brother. The doctor came in during all of this to tell me that I did indeed have the flu. He proceeded to inspect my sinuses and ears as well. Surprise, surprise, I also had an ear infection due to my backed-up sinuses. When my husband found out how bad it was and that our oldest son had been so callous and had ditched me, he said that that was the final straw and our son needed to move out of our home; rock number one in place.

You might be thinking that decision was a bit harsh, but it was just the tip of the iceberg that had been amassing for nineteen years. My husband and I dated for the second half of our senior year of high school. Break-up circumstances aside, I found myself to be one month pregnant two weeks before I graduated. Denial and shame came in like bats out of hell, bloodthirsty and gunning for me.

I became very depressed, having gone from a child to an adult very suddenly. I got a job that I quit when my pregnancy began to show amongst the whispers of my coworkers. I succumbed to an even deeper pit of depression and anger when I found out my ex, now husband, had joined the military and had married someone else and continued on with his life while I was stuck in teen mom hell.

My family didn't really talk about it. Not to my face anyway. People say that your emotions carry over the placenta to the baby, and boy did I have a lot. I still wonder if those emotions infected our son. When he was born, I had a hard time attaching myself emotionally. All I could see was what I'd lost out on in life at the time and the face of his dad. Try carrying that around, plus postpartum depression. I got hit with that hard. I went through counseling, anti-depressant medication, crying, you name it. I worked full time not long after he was born, and I got into college. Thank God my parents supported us during that time. It was a good time of my life, but very hard. My heart was still angry and bitter. I loved my son, but I hated what his existence reminded me of.

He started showing signs of aggression and emotional meltdowns around age two. He was hissing at people, clawing, hitting, etc. We went through many meetings with the school for help. Some help we got. When he was seven years old, he started calling my dad his dad. I had to explain that he was his grandpa and tell him about his real dad and who he was. Somehow, his dad and I established some form of contact. He wanted to meet our son. He and his mom met us at Stone Mountain Park for the day. Our boy was nervous at first, but he then approached, met, and hugged his dad.

We hiked up the side of Stone Mountain on the trail. It was good until lunch, but his meltdowns started to creep in later in the day. His grandma asked right then and there what was wrong with him. I didn't know what to say and still secretly carried a seed of shame and blame in my heart for how he turned out. We went to the playground near the mountain and sat down to rest while our son played. His dad and I talked, and it was as if God had wiped away all of my anger that I'd been harboring toward him. He was going through a divorce. He wanted to see our son more often. He wanted to see me. Long story short, he got divorced a few months later. We ended up dating and got married. Hard place!

After years of not having him around, our dating and subsequent marriage plus our son's behavioral issues, plus his dad's lack of parenting skills, plus family hurt equals Boom! Explosion! Carrying around pain from his past and suddenly becoming a dad to an angry and frustrated kid, married to an in love but bitter and homesick wife did not help my husband. Add in my second pregnancy just two months into our marriage, recent college graduation, a move from my home to another state, and holy moly, Jesus, take the wheel! We were not prepared, not at all!

The next ten years were filled with arguments. He said, she said. One-sided stories and baggage. Fleeting moments of happiness in the mire. I watched the people I loved tear each other apart. Add in feelings from in-laws and my side of the family contributed to the strife, and war erupted. Blaming, yelling, half-truths, tears, poisonous words, and prayers.

It affected us physically, emotionally, and spiritually. By the time February 17 came this year, I'd been on my knees every night at the foot of my children's beds, my bed, and crying out to God for peace in my van, screaming, too.

I called a pastor from our church out of desperation, and he agreed that we should ask our son to leave our home. Our teenage son no longer listened to anyone. He'd scream at me, his dad, his brothers. Nothing mattered. He threatened and bullied us, and it was only worse when his dad was deployed. He got in trouble at school for things he said and ended up suspended with mandatory counseling. Eventually, the police came to our home. After all of this prayer and good counsel, I asked him to come home the day of the emergency room trip to collect his things and move out.

The reality didn't hit until we were both on the doorstep and I handed him his birth certificate. That was gut-wrenching. I chose to let my child go in hopes that God would take hold of him and turn his heart back to Him. My family grumbled, my husband grumbled, I cried and tried to be strong.

Online arguments ensued between father and son. Boundaries were crossed, and confidences were violated. The family grapevine was activated, and I was messaged and called by my family. Everyone wanted me to take sides, lay blame, and fix what I couldn't, what only God could fix. I was stuck between a rock and a hard place. In the linen closet in my bathroom is a massive box of matches. I use them to light candles at night while I indulge in a hot bath and read a book. They are also used to light, blow out, and wave around the smoke to cover up the toilet stench.

Scenario #1: I imagine if I had a fuse while I huddled between that rock and a hard place, I would take that box of matches, strike up a flame, and watch it drop in slow motion from my fingertips. It would ignite the fuse near my cowering feet, and with a flash, an explosion would take away all of the arguing and pain, and the heartbreaking torment would be over.

Scenario #2: I could hand that box of matches over to everyone else and allow them to take me out: Just me.

Scenario #3: I could light a match and take them out. I know what you're probably thinking. Man, she's crazy. Why does every scenario involve someone taken out by fire? When you are stuck that long with the ones you love eating each other alive, it seems a viable option. I know I'm not the only one that has felt this way, nor will I be the last. I want to say that I get it. I get you. You and I are not alone.

God had to remind me of that promise over and over. For those of you hoping for another scenario, preferably a nonviolent option, here you go.

Scenario #4: I realize that all that time and now, I have not been alone. Jesus has been with me all along. I hand Him the box of matches, and he withdraws only one to light a candle and leads me by the hand, or the nose if necessary, out of the darkness. He douses the rest of the matches with water. The crowd surrounding the rock and the hard place disperses in disbelief, dropping their pitchforks and biting comments, dripping with disdain. I leave with Jesus. We go with the light and leave the rest behind in the darkness. They can argue if they want, but I'm letting my Daddy handle things from now on.

Now, imagine being thrown into a furnace for not bowing down to popular opinion. You are lit on fire on purpose for sticking with your beliefs. Now that is between a rock and a hard place. In the book of Daniel, King Nebuchadnezzar of Babylon made an image of himself out of gold to be worshiped by people of every nation and language. This ruler commanded them, with no regard for their personal beliefs, to bow down and worship this man's ego in the form of a golden persona.

How arrogant. How fearsome. How terrifying. How insincere. These people either bowed down or were thrown into a furnace to die. Who does that? Who kills people to stroke his ego, and who the heck keeps human-sized furnaces? Nebuchadnezzar, that's who. The deranged, self-centered, maniacal king of Babylon.

He even had informant tattletales: astrologers. They fussed and boohooed over three individuals, who happened to be Jewish, that the king had appointed over the affairs of Babylon. I may be reaching here, but the devil must have hated the blessings on the Jewish people so badly, that he was petty enough to destroy their witness for God by having those astrologers tell on them in hopes that they'd die.

Isn't that just like the devil? He'll go through people you don't know, or even ones you do know, to kill your witness for Jesus. And if you blow it, then who would want to say yes to God and become a Christian?

These astrologers set the king's heart ablaze with anger so that he summoned Shadrach, Meshach, and Abednego to question them and give them an ultimatum. They could bow down or go into the furnace. This proposition, if you could call it that, was followed by taunts and mockery. His royal pushiness tried provoking them, asking what god could save them.

The boys then answered with some gusto and a whole lot of moxie.

> Shadrach, Meshach, and Abednego replied to him, "King Nebuchadnezzar, we do not need to defend ourselves before you in this matter. If we are thrown into the blazing furnace, the God we serve is able to deliver us from it, and he will deliver us from it, and he will deliver us from your Majesty's hand. But even if he does not, we want you to know, Your Majesty, that we will not serve your gods or worship the image of gold you have set up."
>
> Daniel 3:16–18

Holy mother of boldness! These fellas had backbones of steel and one heck of a faith in God! I can't say I'd have the nerve to say what they said in the presence of someone who had the authority to throw me in a giant oven and make me extra crispy. I have the nerve in much lesser situations, but I usually regret the words that fly from my mouth towards my unsuspecting and perhaps unwilling recipients. But these guys. Man! If they were in a TV drama saying this stuff, I would probably stand to my feet and shout "YES!" with such enthusiasm I'd scare my kids and my dogs while dropping hot buttered popcorn all over the floor, couch, and my children. They would be curled into shocked bundles of arms and legs tucked into their chests at my sudden outburst.

Imagine how God felt. His character was being honored and defended with such passion. What a proud Papa! He'd shout to no one in particular, "Those are my boys!" Heaven would applaud thunderously as God would grin ear to ear and say, "Now, watch this!" He'd disappear from heaven only to reappear next to the swarthy young men the moment they were thrown into the furnace…a furnace that had been heated up seven times hotter than usual, just because the king was ticked off.

The soldiers who threw the three in died because the heat was so intense. Shadrach, Meshach, and Abednego did not. The king saw and questioned how on earth they could not only be alive but untied, walking around, and certainly not alone. A fourth man was seen and was said to look like the son of the gods. Hello! Jesus!

The king was flabbergasted! He shouted for them to come out of the furnace, and his people surrounded them and gawked. They could find no evidence of fire on these young men. Not a singed hair, whiff of smoke, or hole burned by a cinder. Nothing! The king sent out a decree stating that anyone saying anything against the God of Shadrach, Meshach, and Abednego, would be hacked into pieces and have their homes destroyed because there was no other god that could save in this way. Talk about a witness!

So, when you feel like your life is erupting into flames because you lit the match or allowed someone else to, I encourage you to drop it, let it go, and hand the matches over to God. Let Him fight your battles for you while you stay in faith and step back from the mess. Pray constantly and ask for wisdom. Cry. Drink coffee. Work. Work out. But leave the fires to God. He will never leave you nor forsake you. Even if your family and friends might, you are not alone in the fire. Allow God to refine you. Allow Him to pry your pretty little fingers off of that box of matches so he can work on you and the people around you. You are not the Holy Spirit! I'm still learning this in my own family, but God shows me he is big enough. Even when he has to pry my fingers loose, too, with a crowbar at times, He's got this. He's got me. He's got you too.

Healing is taking place in my family. Prayers are coming to fruition. We will be a mighty and unstoppable force for Jesus on this earth! Don't stop believing in your patience and God's timing.

Ring Box

My husband proposed to me eleven years ago while I was in the shower. I was all by my lonesome, minding my beeswax in my birthday suit, when I heard the bathroom door creak open ever so gently. Seconds later, a slip of paper appeared over the top of the shower curtain. I started shaking before even reading the marker scrawled words. "Will you marry me?" I knew what it was going to say. I grabbed the side of the curtain and drew it open a tad, still having a barrier between us of water-soaked vinyl and a cloth shower curtain, asked him if he was serious. He said yes.

If my legs could shake any harder, I probably would have dropped through the tub into the guest bathroom below. I'd only recently confessed to him that I loved him, and here we were in this awkward situation. He was visiting me in Georgia on his way to Tennessee, where his grandpa was very sick, possibly dying.

In my heart, I wanted to say I was not ready. There. Done. Simple. But it wasn't simple. He had an assignment to move to England, and I had my last semester of college to finish. My relationship with Jesus was just starting to deepen. But there was also our son. He had only met his dad a few months prior. We already had bumps and bruises because I was falling in love with Jesus while my then-boyfriend was not. He also had a temper at times. But I loved him anyway.

Not simple at all. Too many emotions and lives were intertwined. I made him promise that everything would be okay.

In retrospect, we both said yes out of naivety. He did not have a ring for me, so we went together to pick one out a few days later. We said our "I do's" in October, 2008 in Lawrenceville, Georgia. Our son and I moved to Florida two months later. Homesickness, isolation, boredom, and pregnancy turned our world upside down. Pure misery hit us all.

We thought we were moving to England. Wrong. Our orders were canceled, and instead, we moved to Little Rock Air Force Base in Jacksonville, Arkansas, where we stayed for three years. More arguing ensued there. By then, our second son was born. My husband and our oldest son were evolving into mortal enemies. How could I love two people who obviously hated each other? Talk about feeling lost. We'd made a promise to each other to love and stay committed in the good and the bad, and here we were, hanging on by a thread. My husband got orders for a six-month deployment to Qatar, and at first, I panicked because I wasn't near any family and had very few friends. Our boys and I would be alone. Utterly alone. When my husband left for Qatar, I drove away from the airport with not one tear on my face. Not a single tear. You may think that's coldhearted, but we were so emotionally pummeled at the time, we just needed a break from each other. This deployment was a godsend. At least that's what I thought.

We had established routines, and all was going well when I began having hot flashes and feeling so sick to my stomach that I thought I'd hurl on my way to our son's school in the morning. Yup, you guessed it. Baby number three was on the way. I was almost thirty years old at the time. I did not, I repeat, I did *not* want another baby, but there I was. I was also ten pounds from my pre-pregnancy weight after my second son. Things were good. Ha! God had other plans. Of course, he did!

I called my husband via skype, crying, and I told him I believed I was pregnant. He chuckled and asked if I was joking. I was not. Our youngest son came into being even though I was on birth control. You're probably thinking, *Silly rabbit, those pills aren't 100% effective*, which I know. There we were, a deployed soldier and his hot mess of a pregnant wife, across the world from one another.

My husband arrived home later that year, greeted at the airport by my six-month pregnant self, our two sons, and his mom, my mother-in-law. Not much later, we received orders to move to Germany. We also received orders to move to Georgia for a special assignment that my husband had applied for.

I love my family tremendously and would have loved moving to Georgia, but Germany tugged at my heart more. I was born there and lived there again as a middle schooler. I have so many good memories there, so that is what we chose. Germany was amazing and horrible at the same time. We found a beautiful old farmhouse at the edge of a quiet village. Our neighbors were so nice, and I taught their daughter art lessons. She was absolutely amazing! Our landlord and his wife treated us like family. They'd come over on Easter and Christmas Eve and would hide chocolates for our boys and bring presents. We adored them!

We were able to travel to Paris a few times as well as Prague and Bavaria. We went to church in Ramstein and a life group on Wednesdays. I went to Bible studies year-round, took German lessons once a week, and our middle son went to kindergarten in our village. We hiked, attended festivals, saw Roman ruins, and more. But the devil still had it out for us, particularly for my husband and our oldest son. They'd have heated arguments. Explosively and repeatedly. Then I'd get half-truths from each of them. We all felt the heat from these battles. They wanted me to take sides, again and again. I prayed privately. I cried in despair. We kept a lot hidden from our friends.

At one point, I truly despised my husband, but when I prayed and asked God who would want someone like him, he said that He did. In fact, for years, God had been trying to get me to hand over my husband to Him. He wanted me to take my hands off the reigns. When pain is all you see, and your heart is scorched, you just want it fixed. You don't want to hand over control at all. Not even by one inch. But God had to change His son, and He had to change me, His daughter.

God has a sense of humor, too. In Arkansas, I remember going on a walk and crying and loudly telling God he could have my husband. I was done trying. Do you know what he said? "Finally!" I must be one tough nut to crack. I persist in holding on at times when I should be letting go. I hold on to the good times. I hold on to the bad. I hold on because I've seen the glimmer of Jesus in my husband's eyes. I know the signs of an attack from the enemy, and I've learned to dig in my heels the most then.

I fall to my knees and pray through tears and anger. I let go, and God doles out the Holy Ghost spankings as he sees fit, not only to my husband but to me. I want us to shed off the prideful and arrogant sludge and be a power couple for Jesus, on fire for Him, and in love with each other. I want us to be a shining example to other couples, so they know they are loved, not alone, and not forgotten, but chosen, treasured, and precious beyond all belief!

Marriage, the whole beautiful mess, is a battlefield. You will fight the fight of your life and hang on and flourish by God's grace, or you won't. I will say, in the case of abuse and or infidelity, God does not expect you to stay. Please, if that is your situation, seek wise counsel and then proceed. Whether you stay or leave, wear your wedding rings or don't, you are loved so unbelievably much by God. That ring box you keep in your closet could symbolize love, hate, adoration, or despair! Thank God that when we are faithless, He is faithful!

I pray that you give Jesus the chance to chase after you like you have chased after love or like you want to be. As if you could stop Him. He is not forceful, but he is persistent, kind, and generous. He would go through hell for you. As a matter of fact, he did. It is hard to think of going through hell willingly for another person. It is crushing to think of sticking around and pursuing the one you love when they spit on your love many times. It is unimaginable to chase after your love, who has demons pulling them down and whispering in their ear that they'd be better off somewhere else, but we do it. We do it because we love them. We do it because we know the truth. We do it because we know the devil hates love and marriage. He would like nothing more than to rip our joy apart and shatter your witness for Christ Jesus into microscopic shards.

Jesus needs us to weather our storms because there is someone in need on the other side of them. We have been sent on a mission to help save the world. This mission means encountering millions of trials and demons. Would you accept this mission knowing that the one you are pursuing and love could be the catalyst to help save millions?

In the book of Luke, Jesus and his disciples crossed over the lake to reach the region of the Gerasenes on the other side. Jesus fell asleep on the voyage, and a dangerous storm developed and began dumping water on board. The disciples flipped out because they thought they were going to drown. They woke Jesus. Jesus rebuked the wind and the raging waters, and the storms subsided. He got onto the disciples about their lack of faith, and they were even more unnerved because this man had just stopped nature from killing them. Mic drop Jesus!

They finished sailing across the sea of Galilee, and when they landed, Jesus stepped ashore. He wasn't greeted by townspeople there, but by a self-mutilated, demon-filled, naked man. That's right. This man was in his birthday suit, filled with self-cutting, mega-strong, isolating, people-rejecting demons.

Many people had tried chaining him up, but he broke the fetters. He fell at the feet of Jesus and screamed. What do want to bet the disciples were probably shaking violently in a huddled mass, wanting to retreat for the hills or back to the boat, especially when the demon gave his name. Storm or not, I bet they wanted to run or swim and get the heck out of the dodge. I would have felt the same. The man screamed at Jesus, fell to his feet, and asked what he wanted with him. To torture him, perhaps?

"Jesus asked him, 'What is your name?' 'Legion,' he replied, because many demons had gone into him" (Luke 8:30). Side note, a legion at the time was around 5,000 soldiers. Can you imagine having 5,000 demons inside of you? My bad days would never compare to that. A bad day for me is when my children are arguing nonstop. My blood boils over. They fight, and then they turn on me. Suddenly I'm the hated one, and they tell me so. The house is a total mess, we are behind on errands, and I'm sick. My husband is deployed. We have soccer practice. I haven't had coffee or a break to be alone and paint, write, read or go to the bathroom in peace because when you have kids, they always know where to find you, and they do.

I sob on the phone to my mom, eat a million cookies, drink coffee, and binge-watch a favorite show, in my bathroom or closet, anywhere with all the doors locked. Horrible. Totally relatable. But still, no matter how I'd like to complain, this is nothing near to even having one demon living inside of you, let alone 5,000, give or take a few, taking up residence.

Jesus gave these demons permission to enter a herd of swine, who then drowned themselves in the lake. The pig herdsman told the town. The town came running. Jesus and the no longer crazy man were calmly sitting together. And oh yeah, the man was clothed and in his right mind. These people, who had known how the man was before, all of them, asked Jesus to leave. You might be agreeing with them or scratching your head at this point. If I knew a local crazy, violent, naked, homeless man had been suddenly set free, I'd want to find out how.

Notice: when you go through hell for the one you promised your life to because you know the promise within them was one or a million breakthroughs away, you will have loved ones, close friends, coworkers, and more that want you out of their life. They can't handle seeing such love overcome such drama. Meanwhile, the one that put the ring on your finger will want to run and tell the world! You may be the only Jesus they will ever see in their life. You may be the only one willing to dive into the mess of loving them, no matter the cost. I encourage you to put your toes in those waters and take the plunge, even if those waters are shark-infested.

It may feel like you're drowning, but you're not. It may feel like you're alone, but you're not. The days will feel long and the nights even longer, but *do not give up!* Where humans may fail, where ring boxes may close, your Father in heaven will pursue you through time with an everlasting love.

> "The Lord appeared to me (Israel) from ages past, saying, 'I have loved you with an everlasting love: Therefore, with lovingkindness I have drawn you and continued my faithfulness to you'" (Jeremiah 31:3, AMP).

The Empty Box

I haven't been able to write for a week. It's not like I haven't wanted to, but at each attempt, I became disgustingly overwhelmed with the lack of ideas in my hands. The endeavor is there, but my pages have remained empty. Part of me has wanted to cry because I know what I'm capable of doing, but the will and desire seem to have grabbed a latte and strolled on out of here, leaving a shell of myself behind.

I've got a 48x60 canvas I have been working on, plus this book, plus writing and illustrating amazing children's books, but lately, these pleasures taste like ash in my mouth. I've also been teaching myself some French. Pair this with two sons with cabin fever over summer break, a husband that took two weeks of leave from work, and the never-ending allergy issue I have to the place that I live, my time of the month going whacko, and you have a mess.

Aunt Flo comes and goes as she very well pleases and leaves me a sobbing, snapping, joyless momma bear on the verge of a breakdown. Part of me hates not feeling a sense of direction for my gifts and talents. Another part of me says, "Hallelujah, I can sit on the couch and watch a movie or binge on a season of whatever is currently striking my fancy like baking shows from England, superhero stories, or murder mysteries. I've found myself up past midnight watching military homecoming videos, comedians, or sometimes animal rescue and rehabilitation videos. I'm a total sap, so I cry at each one.

Laughing feels rare, and time seems never to be enough. Dishes get done and laundry too, but I just feel so lost, empty, and dissatisfied. I find myself wondering why: Why do I feel like a ship with no course? Why do I feel like I have no purpose? Why do I feel so invisible? Why do I want to conquer the world with paintings, books, and inspirational works, but I feel so bitter and lost?

Maybe my focus is off Jesus and on myself too much. Maybe it is my hormones. Maybe it is me taking on too much and not allowing God to be God. I do that a lot. I'm not gonna lie. Maybe I'm so revved up at the possibilities because God has something amazing for me, but it just isn't my launch time. Maybe.

Maybe is such an ugly word. Maybe I'll work out today. Maybe I'll clean the house. Maybe I'll send my book to a publisher. Maybe I'll learn French. Maybe I'll illustrate another book. Maybe I'll eat cleaner foods. Maybe I'll finish my giant painting. Maybe I'll actually make something of myself and profit off of my talents. Maybe I'll lose my stressed-out momma belly and finally see abs.

Maybe I'll get a pixie cut. Maybe I'll actually try karaoke because I love singing, but I'm scared senseless of crowds. It took me forever to record myself and share my singing online even though I belt it out at church, in the van, around the house, and when I walk my dogs. I've even created several silly songs for my sons that have them cracking up and smiling along with me.

That's the thing about maybe. It fires up the desires but kills them in their tracks when I don't actually act on them. I'd like to take all of those maybes and shove them into an empty box and say the heck with them. I have quite a lot of empty boxes just waiting to be filled up. However, I think it is time that I kick those empty boxes to the curb.

I can't imagine God enjoys watching his baby girl move her hopes and dreams and abilities into an empty box, no matter how beautiful the thing is. Gilded, painted, mechanical, or voice-activated, I shouldn't squash my soul and smother it with fear and doubt and shove it into a forgotten box that will probably end up on top of a shelf in my closet pushed toward the very back, and collecting dust.

I imagine a future of regret. I'd run into old friends who knew me before I lost myself, and they'd ask me how my art was going. I'd tell them it became just a hobby because people were cheap. Their countenance would fall a bit before another smile would light up their faces, and they'd mention my writing. I'd tell them again how it, like my art, fizzled out and how I just write for myself. At that, they'd nod their heads, mutter an excuse to leave. I'd be left there standing and thinking about that empty box I had filled with pathetic excuses and maybes about my life and who I could have been. The coffin would be nailed shut and the future bleak, and probably without coffee. This girl needs her coffee.

Let's face it. That sounds like death to me. And maybe that's what it is. A death to self. A death to pride. A death to not relying on God and not accepting who He says I am and when I am. Yeah, let's call it that.

I don't know about you, but I don't plan on dying today or anytime soon. Not physically, emotionally, and certainly not spiritually. I know God has a plan for me, and it does not involve me having a pity party and not daring to be everything he created me to be and more.

I vote on taking that box and dumping out all of that silliness. It is time to live, create, and be me again. It is time for you to be yourself too. It is time to pour out the worries and the anxieties and all of the what-ifs. We may cry or even scream, but it is okay. God is bigger than our problems, and

He can take this. He can brace and handle us. He is strong enough even when we are not. God can handle all of you. He made you. He can fix you and fill you with hope and purpose again.

> I, the Lord, have called you in righteous-
> ness; I will take hold of your hand. I
> will keep you and will make you to be
> a covenant for the people and a light for
> the Gentiles, to open the eyes that are
> blind, to free captives from prison and to
> release from the dungeon those who sit
> in darkness.
>
> Isaiah 42:6–7

In the book of Luke, there was a broken woman who came to anoint Jesus, a sinful woman as the Pharisees called her. She entered the house of a Pharisee and walked past everyone, all men, straight to Jesus. All eyes were on her, and whispers began to circulate. She strode with intention toward the only one in the room whose eyes weren't full of distaste or anger but of compassion and love. She stood silently weeping behind Jesus with an alabaster jar of perfume in her hands.

The men around Jesus were appalled and disgusted as this woman knelt, crying over the feet of Jesus, pouring out the costly oil upon his feet. She went a step further and wiped his feet clean with her hair and kissed them. Jesus not only allowed her to touch him in a personal and intimate way but stood up for her against the spiteful hatred dripping from the lips of a Pharisee nearby.

> "Two people owed money to a certain
> money lender. One owed him five hun-

> dred denarii, and the other fifty. Neither
> of them had the money to pay him back,
> so he forgave the debts of both. Now
> which of them will love him more?"
> Simon replied, "I suppose the one who
> had the bigger debt forgiven." "You have
> judged correctly," Jesus said.
>
> Luke 7:41–43

Jesus went one step ahead and turned toward the woman but talked to Simon. He was bold.

> "Do you see this woman? I came into
> your house. You did not give me any
> water for my feet, but she wet my feet
> with her tears and wiped them with her
> hair. You did not give me a kiss, but this
> woman, from the time I entered, has not
> stopped kissing my feet. You did not put
> oil on my head, but she poured out per-
> fume on my feet. Therefore, I tell you,
> her many sins have been forgiven—as her
> great love has shown. But whoever has
> been forgiven little loves little"
>
> Luke 7:44–47

Bam, Jesus! What a moment of truth and redemption! Jesus went another step and told her that her sins were
forgiven. The Pharisees must have looked like some pur-
ple-faced, choked out, highfalutin know-it-alls, a little too
big for their britches at the moment and feeling like chided
school children. And yet, Jesus loved them too. How much
He wanted all of his children free and forgiven.

The other guests began to murmur as well. They were just as baffled because, as far as they knew, only God could forgive sins. Little did they know that the Almighty was sitting in the room right before their eyes, setting their religious behinds straight. And, oh my goodness, for the cherry on top, Jesus tells the woman, whose mouth probably flew wide open in disbelief herself, that her faith has saved her and to go in peace.

This woman, this beautiful daughter, took what was expensive and important to herself and made a decision to pour it out on someone else in a lavish show of love and adoration. It was a sacrifice, an anointing on Jesus, and a bowing of her knee to her Savior and King. Could anything be more beautiful than to give back to the one who has given everything to you?

She gave up her what-ifs, fears, inadequacies, indulgences, and presumptions about her life to the only one who could fill her up with life and purpose. She had to break open her box, her life, for something beautiful to pour out. She dared to reach for something more, for someone more, to be more. She didn't care who watched. She didn't care about the tittle-tattle. The ice-cold stares evaporated before ever piercing her skin. She'd been through too much already. She was ready to pour herself out, to be reassembled, redefined, and repurposed.

My goodness, the afterglow she must have worn after receiving forgiveness and peace for acting on what her spirit had driven her to. I bet it knocked the socks off of those Pharisees if they'd worn any. Just go with it.

As sinful as she was, this woman bravely brought her empty box to the King in the presence of a religious audience. Come hell or high water; she was on a mission.

No one was gonna stop her. I know that desperation. I know the depressing, sinking feeling when you think your purpose may never come to fruition. You think you'll never make a difference in this world because you feel invisible, unnecessary, unappreciated. Your cries to be seen, to feel wanted and worthy, seem to bounce off the empty canyon walls of your life. One moment you feel like you're on top of the world and ready to ignite a revolution with your God-given gifts, then you are there, alone, storing them away in your box. Whose lives are on the line if you don't take those gems of purpose out of hiding and set them into the crown of purpose meant for you to wear? Who would be kept in the dark because you lacked the nerve, the moxie, the gumption to be everything God made you to be?

In Persia, somewhere between 460 and 350 BC, Esther, a Jewish girl turned woman, became the wife of King Xerxes. He is the same king that ruled over 127 provinces, reaching from India to Cush. Now that's a man with some power! For 180 days, King Xerxes displayed his wealth and majesty. He held a banquet lasting seven days. Who does that? You'd definitely need your stretchy pants because the spread of delicacies, wine, and sweets would be astronomical. I can't even imagine. Good grief, Thanksgiving day's food is enough to make me satisfied and simultaneously sick to my stomach. These fellas who attended must have had a non-GMO, organic, free-range, grass-fed, finger-licking good feast the size of Texas and an unvarnished, pristine, high-octane engine-fueled metabolism of a teenager to survive this event.

At the time, Xerxes had a different queen. Queen Vashti held her own feast away from the men and refused to make an appearance just to be gawked at and leered over by stuffed, drunken, debaucherous men. Smart girl, in my opinion. However, according to the laws at the time, telling

Hubby Xerxes a big fat no in response to his summons was not only a crime but a monstrous slap to his egotistical face and pride and would potentially incite a rebellion in women everywhere to disrespect and dishonor their husbands. Yup, she was that girl.

It must have stung pretty badly because Xerxes declared Vashti Queen no more and began searching for a new queen. Enter Hadassah, a Hebrew woman, using the name Esther.

She and many other beautiful women were rounded up like cattle and placed into the king's harem for beauty treatments until such a time as the king would select a new bride.

But don't you know, God already had a plan: Esther became favored by the king's eunuch Hegai. She pleased him, and he rewarded her with beauty treatments and special foods. She got seven attendants to wait upon her, and they were moved together into the best place in the harem.

Talk about being blessed and pampered. Esther had inside help from her Creator and the king's eunuch. Ladies, how would you like to be set up like this? Spa treatments including oil and myrrh, perfumes and cosmetics for a year! That's right, girls: a year. A year of no worries. A year of living in a penthouse and not having to handle a single load of laundry, no cooking required, no running errands and playing taxi, nada, just pure bliss.

And wouldn't you know, after all of this, chosen over Lord knows how many other women, Xerxes picked Esther. He thought she was stunningly beautiful, and he just had to have her. He laid a crown on her head while removing it from Vashti. Goodbye small-town girl, hello Queen Esther, co-ruler over 127 provinces. A great banquet was to follow in her honor. The king even proclaimed a holiday throughout all of their provinces while distributing gifts profusely with style and panache and perhaps glittering in gold.

Esther was the queen, but she had yet to reveal who she truly was. She was still a Jew named Hadassah from Susa. She gained all the prestige and power but still clutched at anonymity out of fear of who she truly was. What a pity to deny who you truly are because you'd rather maintain the façade you've donned for someone else's pleasure, at the cost of the duality of your soul.

She shoved her empty box full of what-ifs. What if someone found out who she was. Would they hate her? Would they love to embrace her? Would they kill her? I've got to admit; if I were in her shoes, with rising hostility between nations at the and the threat of mass genocide looming, I'd be scared out of my mind. I'd probably hide who I was too. But doing so eats away at you every day, and piece after piece floats away as you crumble into a pile of ashes: sad, faded, and gray. You become a shell of who you could be, and for what?

There comes a time when you will no longer take the threats of a bullying spirit of fear. You won't bow the knee to those what-ifs and that empty box. Not any longer. At this point, you have a choice. Stay hidden, potentially in danger, and miserable, or you take a stand, no matter the cost. You let God take you by the hand, and you stand, baby girl. You *stand*! No more hiding, no more cowering, just utter gall, gumption, and nerves of steel!

Esther stood up to her fear. In a time when her husband could annihilate her people, she had a choice to make. She could remain silent and hide who she truly was, or she could step forward and reveal herself as the daughter of the most-high God and present herself to her husband, the king, unbidden. Her people's lives were on the line. S God could raise someone else to stand in the gap for her people, but why not Esther? Perhaps she was born for such a time as this.

This woman, this queen, this precious girl from the tribe of Benjamin, made a choice.

She kicked fear to the curb and went into the presence of the king. She could have died if he had not accepted her approach, but he showed her favor. Esther chose this moment to invite him to a banquet and another, and then she revealed who she truly was. She was part of the very people the king had permitted to destroy because a liar whispered in his ear falsehoods of the worthlessness of the entire nation.

Haman had spewed hate from personal bitterness into the mind of Xerxes and nearly brainwashed the king into committing genocide. I imagine when the Jews were finally able to defend themselves, and Haman was hanged for his plotting, the devil was writhing with fury and screaming into deaf ears perturbance of his foiled plan.

Don't you know that's what he does when a believer refuses to buy into his well thought out schemes? Girl, you go ahead and drop the hammer on that scaly, no good, troglodyte. Tell him to slither on back to the cave from whence he came and not ever to return. You stand tall in who you are and who He made you. Go ahead and dump out that box of what-ifs. Empty it out, kick it away from your person with some gusto, and you go ahead and hope, make a change, and leap into who God says you are!

The Gift Box

About two months ago, I was at a low point. I felt unseen, unimportant, rejected, and overlooked. People admired my gifts, but my source of income was drying up. My paintings were not selling regularly anymore. At the time, I was raising golden retriever puppies too. Our second litter of pups was our last one because, while doing the right thing to make sure the parents did not have any health concerns, I discovered our male, the sire, had mild hip dysplasia, a genetic condition that can pass on to the babies. The second delivery of pups was a traumatic experience. Our girl had birthed eight pups at home before she couldn't push anymore. Her body gave out. I called the vet and brought her and her newborns. I was able to pick her up the next day after a phone call that broke my heart.

Two of her boys were stuck in her and deprived of air too long. They were not alive when she was able to push them out. The vet said there were three more. I had a glimmer of hope. He said that the girls' sacks had burst inside of momma, and they had lesions on their skin. The vet tried reviving them. They did everything they could, but we lost the babies.

I cried and blamed myself all the way to get our girl and her babies and bring them home. Emma, our momma golden retriever, looked so empty, haunted even. I took her home with the eight babies we still had. She didn't really seem all that interested in them after her C-section. I watched her grieve. Despite this, the babies grew well, and Emma was the best mother.

I had a bitter taste in my mouth as yet another effort to make income was stripped away. I tried and tried but was turned down over and over in selling my art or getting commissions. At the time, I didn't understand. I assumed that because I had these God-given gifts, I could use them how and when I wanted to provide income for our family. With or without God's blessing and prompting, I went ahead, based on my feelings.

With the income dwindling and emotions flying at home and in my head. I felt stripped bare and naked to boot. I worked my mind into a frenzy about the why of it all. God didn't say much, but He has convicted me before that He is my provider and my husband is not. Faced with the ever-present thoughts flung my way, God asked me one day while I was driving and feeling worthless, "Who told you that?"

It shook me. I'd been relying on people to validate me and not on God. Oh, I knew it had to come from God, but I kept reverting to affirmation from home and from people online in my art groups, people whom I had never met in person.

I prayed and cried, and I yelled at God. I yelled at God a lot. I cried and prayed some more but still, no reprieve or answer. I sought comfort in phone calls from friends and my parents to keep me propped up. I watched sermon after sermon online to tell me what I wanted to hear. I blasted worship music around the house and in the van and went to Wednesday prayer and worship at noon. I binged shows online nonstop, usually involving a love story or a baking show, all to fill the hole that was never going to be satisfied with anything or anyone other than Jesus.

I declared things in faith about my art, books, and songs, all the while not asking God what He thought or seeking His approval until I was already into a project or finished while desperately desiring support from my husband, that did not come. His ideas of success and mine were and are vastly different.

My time became very unfruitful and out of balance. I spent most of it trying to chase away the ache of emptiness, loneliness, bitterness, anger, rejection, and more. I tried being everything to everyone and found by human standards that it was not enough.

I have more books than you can imagine to help prop me up again. They covered the back of my toilet and counter along with one or two translations of the Bible. They were books on battling your thoughts, prayer, never giving up, my identity in Christ, and more. I'd read a little of one and move to another, never finishing them. There were more in my closet, bedroom, dining room, van, and even in a random backpack leftover from a trip, as well as my art studio.

This collection does not include the many Bible studies I did at home and church. I isolated myself with the word of God without letting it work through me until it all came to a head at church one day, and I cracked. A few days prior, I'd been falling to my knees during workouts and breaking out in uncontrollable sobs. I had no idea what was going on. I thought it was some horrid ingredient in my pre-workout formula affecting me. My periods were off cycle. My moods were, well, moody. I hadn't genuinely smiled in God knows how long. I was just a shell.

I talked it over with my mom, who is a wealth of information, seeing as how she's been a registered nurse for some thirty-plus years. I did not, I repeat, I DID NOT, want to go to women's health on base for a checkup because, in my family, ovarian cancer and more have gotten a hold of members.

I was so weepy and stressed with life in general and not feeling valued, so when the invitation for prayer came at church for those that felt like I did, I stood, no questions asked, probably to the shock of my husband, who was right next to me. People surrounded me, and laid hands on me, and prayed along with the pastor. I silently let tears run down my cheeks during it all. I was exposed. I was vulnerable and laid bare before our congregation, God, and the devil.

The next day I broke down, and I mean, broke down. Anxiety hit hard out of nowhere, and I finally went to the base clinic to talk to someone in women's health and rule out any physical possibilities. My doctor was very sweet as she took in my overwhelmed self, shaking and crying. She said, "We can do tests, but I think you know that this is stress-related."

She performed a pelvic exam, which was normal. She ordered a pull panel of blood tests and a pelvic ultrasound. They checked my thyroid, cortisol levels, and more. The woman who drew my blood was none too gentle as she did it.

The doctor sent my lab work to somewhere in Texas. They came back fine, all normal. Just as I suspected because God had healed my thyroid before. My cortisol levels were normal too. That I did not expect. My pelvic ultrasound revealed something, but they didn't know what it was. She ordered an MRI and more labs. More poking and prodding I did not understand. I scheduled the MRI and had to wait a few weeks.

In the meantime, suicidal thoughts attacked my mind at night and throughout the day. Anxiety came too, and fear in general. I knew this was not physical, but spiritual. Going to bed was a nightmare! At this point, I stopped taking pre-workout supplements too, which seemed to help some in not feeling so anxious, but the thoughts persisted. Another opportunity for prayer came in church when our pastor said God told him people in the congregation were under attacks of fear. He had us stand to have hands laid on us and prayers spoken. After that night, it got so much worse.

My joy and peace began draining. I didn't want to do Bible study because whatever I read became a weapon for the enemy to discredit God's nature based on some Old Testament verses out of context. The devil spoke lies and suggestions in my mind about God not being good, loving, or caring. He snatched truth and replaced it with fear, lovelessness, and lies, which made God sound callous and uncaring. I put that book away and started another study.

In all this, my children were oblivious. My husband has had to watch his wife melt away almost overnight. He saw my personality evaporate and be replaced with fear and trembling. Crying. Panic attacks. Nightmares of the devil trying to choke me out from behind, to silence my voice, while he smiled. I must have actually cried out because my husband woke me and held me like a frightened and weeping child in his arms.

I walked around nervous, scared, and with no appetite eventually. I began losing weight. Not because I wanted to, but food brought no pleasure. When I would attempt eating, my gag reflex kicked in. I felt like throwing up, but my mind and spirit held on. I made myself drink meal replacement shakes instead to force nutrition.

I rolled my ankle off a step during exercise, and the pain persisted for over two months. Since I had not been taking pre-workout, I was so much weaker. But I continued exercising, and my strength grew. I maintained the same schedule taking care of the kids, the dogs, myself, housework, but my enthusiasm began to dwindle until only a flicker remained.

Then numbness set in. I didn't want to paint, write, or do anything I had enjoyed before. Movies became pointless and began to overwhelm me, so I stopped watching them. I could barely read for enjoyment anymore. I began feeling dread before sleep to the point I started using melatonin supplements plus magnesium supplements to help me sleep.

Getting out of bed became a chore. I'd wake panicked and sweating, unable to get up because I felt scared for no reason and like I had no purpose. I didn't want to touch or be touched by my husband or my kids. The idea of staying in the house was frightening and without peace, but suddenly, leaving and being in public became petrifying.

Little sounds got to me. Anyone arguing got to me. Loud noises would turn me into a mess. I cried. The Lord knows, I cried. I felt so alone even when surrounded by people. Nothing edified my soul. I began reaching out to friends and followed their advice. I prayed, sought the Lord, and hunted and picked through Scripture. I sang. I forced myself to sing.

I rebuked the devil, but the attacks still came. In all this, as terrible as it has been, God was with me. I've had to throw myself fully into His arms even though I couldn't feel them and trust Him. I had to learn to trust Him. He is fighting for me indeed, and everything is going to be okay. It is okay. I began hearing Him speak to me more than I ever have in my life. For the first time, He told me it was time for me to walk out my faith. The second time I heard Him, He said to choose this day whom you will serve. A while ago, He gave me two words: timing and obedience.

I'd cry and ask Him why, but He didn't tell me. He wanted my trust. In the midst of the worst of it, He said,

"Be at peace." One morning during a panic attack, he quoted Scripture to me. "But they that wait upon the Lord shall renew their strength; they shall mount up with wings as eagles; they shall run and not be weary; and they shall walk and not faint" (Isaiah 40:31, KJV).

Then he quoted Galatians 6:9, "Let us not become weary in doing good, for at the proper time we will reap a harvest if we do not give up." After that I laid in bed for a while, less panicked at first, but it increased. Then He said, "You need to get up and go."

I took it as a prompt to get up and out of bed because of those messy thoughts, but I questioned Him further. Did it mean time to move in my gift? He did not answer. One morning I laid in bed again, having a hard time, and I asked Him what was going on. He said that I'd been living for the approval of man. A few weeks before, when I was broiling over financial issues because of my husband's spending, God got a bit flustered and said, "Don't you know I'm bigger than your husband?" I was not used to Him talking like that.

The morning of the approval comment, I got up and got dressed. I got the kids to school. Man, I didn't want to do that or anything. I cleaned the house and my boys' room. That room was a feat in and of itself because of the massive amount of Legos, trash, clothes, and book everywhere. Then I felt that the Lord wanted me to get on each bed and pray. So, I did. I quietly prayed for all of my boys, even my oldest off at welding school in Texas.

As I quieted myself down, I heard God say, "Woman, thou art loosed!" God went old school King James version on me, I knew it was in the Bible, so I googled it. Luke 13:12 shares the story of a woman who had a spirit of infirmity that kept her bent over for eighteen years. Jesus was teaching on the Sabbath in a synagogue when in came this precious woman. First, he declared she was loosed, then he laid his hands on her, and she was able to stand up and praise God. When I tell you I shouted, I *shouted*! I thanked Him and spoke in tongues. My worship startled my dogs. When I'm that loud worshipping, it usually does. I was on cloud nine before lies came to try to convince me I was not free. But God said I am, so I am. I made a space in my closet for prayer and began to see a breakthrough.

One day, after meeting a new friend who encouraged me to ask God about everything, God told me to watch a movie, so I did. I tried settling down in my comfy bed in my pajamas at 4 p.m. My husband came home and wanted to say hi and get and give affection. My movie started, and the couple on screen argued nonstop. I panicked. I didn't want someone touching me. I could see the hurt on my husband's face as he left the room. This movie was too tense. I asked God why I felt so frantic, and He said it was anger. All of these years of that anger flying around my home made my family and me a hot mess. I went to my husband, and he looked hurt. I felt like a burden because I knew he needed affection, but I could not give it to him. I opened up, and so did he, and years of baggage, pain, and grief flooded out. We both cried. We opened our eyes to the reality we were both hiding and ignoring. Chains that held our marriage hostage were exposed and broken that night.

God's answer to him when he asked what he could do for our family was to buy a boat to get our family out and about. He admitted his addiction to video games and said he was going to change that. This was a new chapter in our family. Since then, he's stood by me. He's begun praying out loud for me and vice versa.

We went to the lake to test the boat with the current owners. It wouldn't start. I thought maybe it was divine intervention, and we weren't supposed to have it. Come to find out; it was a loose wire: a simple fix. My moods were up, then down, then up, then numb and anxious. I fessed up to the owners about it because I could not get out of the truck. The wife told me she knew all about that. She had been on medication for anxiety. When we got on the water, I told her everything. She told me about her nephew who came to her for help but committed suicide. She was teary-eyed and hugged me. She offered prayer and her phone number.

She told me that she prayed with her classroom that our family would be the ones to buy the boat and for it to help us. At the same time, my husband had prayed for God's help, and God told him to get a boat. I got into the water after that, in the middle of Ute lake in New Mexico. Everything was beautiful, and although I felt panicky, I stayed. I believe God wanted to show me how much he had me in his hand. I was safe. He knew I needed it.

After climbing back into the boat, the owner said, "Why don't you get up here and drive." Ha! Way to go, God. He knew I needed that too. We bumped along on choppy water, and I could not close my eyes to God's beauty in nature because I was the driver. On the way home, I was able to talk to my mom back home in Georgia. She was so proud of me. Never underestimate the power of a mother's love! She encouraged me so much! A few nights prior, we had a magnificent thunderstorm. I was feeling condemned, like I had brought all of this down on myself. And in a moment, God called me by my name. He said, "Andrea, neither do I condemn you!"

I gulped back a sob because He knew I needed that. I stepped out of the truck and saw the storm in full effect. The thought came that this was the mighty battle God was fighting for me, not the angels bowling as my mom told me when a kid so I would not be scared during a storm. Sometimes you just need to see something in the waiting to be reassured that God does indeed have you in the palm of His hand and His heart.

I went home and sat out back and watched the storm in awe. It was indeed like a battle as if cannons were firing and explosions of light shattered the darkness. For the first time in about two months, I picked up my pen to write and describe how magnificent it was.

Today I struggled again to get up. But I did. As I did, joy crept in. It was suggested to me to join a partnership class at church in order to serve. I squirmed in my seat, wondering what I was doing there. Would they even want me, a person so broken at that moment? In the end, when everyone left but the instructors, I unloaded my mess. The woman immediately said, "This stops today." She gathered more help and one of the pastors to pray. They told me about my believer's authority as a Christian to squash the devil at his onset, prayed for me, had me pray out confessions, and gave me a book to help me know my rights. It was a divine appointment. They told me to go to the room next door for a talk with people gifted in the prophetic. I didn't have to tell them anything but my name. They prayed and what came out of them made me cry.

They said I was an oak tree in a season. I'd lost things, but they would come back. I would come back, looking the same on the outside but completely different on the inside. I cried because I knew this was happening. I cried and laughed because God showed me a massive and glorious oak tree on a hill with the sun shining brilliantly behind it just a few days before. A few months ago, I got an acorn pendant, and it was so tiny, but I heard in my spirit not to despise small beginnings. God told one of the people there a chapter in Job to read. Again, I laughed because I'd been telling my husband about how Job lost everything, but in the end, God blessed him with double portions of all he'd lost.

I saw a beautiful friend of mine after that in the lobby, serving as a greeter. She is like another mom to me. We talked, cried, hugged, repeated, and she gave me her phone number and said to call whenever. She would come for coffee, meet up, and talk: anything I needed. I met with another woman after that, and she shared her testimony. The same help came and advice and a promise to be available for calls, visits, whatever I needed. I was so light feeling and smiling. I went home and was able to sit and read and have coffee.

I wrote out note cards and wanted to write this chapter, but I couldn't. I sat with my boys through burgers and a movie. It wasn't until my youngest son came into the house later from being on the trampoline. His brother had somehow kicked him in the kneecap. He was crying so loud, which made my dogs cry too. They are sympathy howlers. I sat my son on the counter, got him an ice pack, and carried him to his room. I had him slide over on his bed from me. I curled up on that bottom bunk with him in my arms, and I sang softly to him. This was after him flipping out in the kitchen over the pain and not thinking he'd make it to school. I prayed for his knee. As I sang, I gently switched to praying in tongues. That caught my boy's attention. He asked me what I was saying, and I told him I didn't know. God gave me the language. He said, "You keep saying the same things."

I said that it must be important then. He asked if it was Japanese. I chuckled and said, "Nope."

As I held him and calmed him, I had a moment of perfect clarity for how God has had me all along. Like it or not, God has brought me gifts in this mess. So did the devil.

I prayed for God's gift to refine me. The enemy took that moment to pile on his heavy gifts to interfere.

I'm not the only one to have experienced this. My gift to you is to know that you're not alone. Circumstances may say so, but it is not true. Many times, when God sends a gift, the opposition does the same to discourage you. Don't buy the lies. Reach out, find help, and talk to God. Let Him lead you. Accept the gift of Jesus and what he has done for you. Don't isolate yourself or think you asked for the mess.

You're worth so much to God. You're valuable. Jesus paid the price for you because you are precious and loved. There is a plan for your life, created by God for a hope and a future. You are not alone, and you are so very loved. Someone else needs to hear your testimony. I pray for peace for you in the storm, God's peace. I pray for no fear in the name of Jesus. Lean into Jesus. It takes God, you, and a village. Let there be no shame or condemnation. You are a gift. Let God tell you that. Let Him love you into wholeness. Be blessed!

Coupon Box

My mom used to have the prettiest cream-colored coupon box when I was a kid. It was full of the coolest coupons she would clip from the Sunday paper. She had them all tucked in dividers in alphabetical order. We had the best time on Sundays, raiding the newspaper and clipping out the coupons she selected. This was, of course, after I had removed the funny pages. That right there dates me. Oh well.

I didn't fully understand at the time why we needed the coupons, but I learned later. My dad was in the air force, and with three kids, my parents were pretty frugal. They saved money where they could. My mom found all of the deals and shopped within their means. She told me years later how she'd do what is now called extreme couponing. She would go late at night while my sisters and I were at home sleeping. Now there are TV shows about the very same thing. She never stockpiled what she bought with her coupons but only got what we needed. I cherish the memory of that box and the coupons. They seemed to be magical because we got more for less. Then we would find out how much we had saved and became ecstatic! We got the same product but for less. hallelujah!

How many of you would change your tune if it were you being purchased and your happy behind was placed on a conveyor belt, and the person shopping whipped out coupons, mounds of them, and dumped them on the counter.

You get scanned by the cashier, and then the coupons are added. As you watch, your value begins to depreciate with every beep of the register, and the extra coupons astronomically add up.

Suddenly you're not feeling so hot. The shopper shouts for glee as they get you for nothing. Actually, the cashier has to pay the shopper money. How would you like them apples?

You are lifted unceremoniously off of the conveyor belt and plunked into a shopping cart two sizes too small. Your limbs are folded up like a pretzel, and you are in some serious pain, physically and emotionally. Then the cart is pushed outside over a bumpy parking lot that sets your teeth on edge with vibration, possibly grinding them down to nubs.

When you think you can't handle it anymore, the cart stops in front of the smallest vehicle. You are once again lifted and pushed, shoved, crammed, and slammed into an unbearably tiny trunk. The lid is closed, and there you are, in the dark, rumbling down the road to who knows where. After what seems like an eternity, the car comes to a screeching halt. Blinding light floods the trunk as it flies open, and you are carried into a house full of shelf upon shelf, and hold up, there are more copies of you!

So many replicas of yourself turn bewildered eyes towards you as you're shelved away with them. The shopper is so proud of the deal they got, surveying their loot before turning off the light and closing the door. Wait just a minute. What just happened?

You sit there trying not to be overcome by the dark. You wonder why this happened. You think," I know I'm not this cheap. Why am I here?" Eventually, you are there for so long doubt creeps in. *Maybe I am cheap, worthless. Maybe I should just stay here. I'll make myself as comfy as I can. It isn't so bad.* But your heart sinks, then begins to skip beats. You pour sweat, thinking that this is it. No one values me, and I'm all alone. Time passes and you wallow. How pitiful and pathetic you must be. At this moment, your head hangs in defeat, but you have the strongest urge to look towards the door. You notice a tiny sliver of light coming through a crack.

This whole time you thought you were trapped without hope, and yet here is this door you thought was shut, open. A flutter begins in your chest. You uncurl yourself from the fetal position and tentatively place a foot on the ground. You shudder a bit with that first step, but then you realize you are standing. Hope begins to bubble up, and you take another step and then another. Stiff and pained muscles that have been cramped for so long start to loosen as you move. Your stride becomes more surefooted as you pick up the pace and, before you know it, you're at the door. You reach a shaky hand toward the knob, take in a shaky breath, and push.

Light, peace, love, and freedom all pour into the room and flow through you with hurricane force. You quiver at the newness. These feelings are foreign now; you've forgotten how they touch your soul. You don't know how to handle this happiness. You almost retreat into the darkness, but for a whisper of your name, which barely tickles your ears. You shut your eyes because you're afraid to hope. A gentle hand touches your shoulder, and you open your eyes to see Jesus before you.

You're back at the store, and He's paying for you, but not with coupons. He's exchanged Himself for you so you can walk out free. You try to argue with Him, but He won't allow any protest. Not one bit. Your eyes tear up, and you just can't believe what He's done. He was willing to trade places with you. He paid for you in full, and you didn't have to do a thing but accept it and believe it. He tells you that it's okay, and you can go free now. You look at Him, then look at the door, back at Him, and then your head lifts high, and you walk proudly out of the store into freedom.

What kind of love does that? The love of Christ, that's the kind. He paid the price for our sins in full. He didn't require us to be perfect. We didn't have to have our life in order. He reached into dark pits for us and rescued us anyway. He whispered love songs over us while we curled up in tears we couldn't explain. He sent people to love us and pray for us at our worst moments when we didn't know how to love ourselves. He helped us to stand when we didn't know if our legs would hold us anymore.

He surrounded us with friends when we felt most alone. These friends came and blessed us with encouragement, hugs, love, scriptures, help, and hands to hold when we wanted to collapse into despair. We cried out for a word of hope when we were lonely, and He spoke gently in the night of how He was doing a new thing in us.

Oh, darling, I know too well how this feels. God has been walking with me through a season of an unexpected and intense bout of depression and anxiety. He still is walking through this with me, and I have hope in Him. When I couldn't hear Him speak, He sent women to lift me up at Bible study. When I felt overwhelmed and had panic attacks at work, He sent co-workers to talk calmly. He sent an usher or two at church to pray over me or hold my hand during an anxiety attack as I laid on a couch in the lobby with tears streaming down my face.

When I felt I couldn't breathe and was so very broken, He sent a friend through an online art group across the world to talk me through. She sent me a link to a sermon online that spoke of planting the seed of God's word into my heart. That, in turn, lead to another video on health in our bodies and minds and healing through Jesus. As I spoke and aligned my heart with God's word, the pain in the back of my head from anxiety left. The more I prayed and believed in my healing that Jesus already died to give me, the more peace I felt. Freedom was breaking into my heart. I've been on this road for a long time and am still traveling, but I am not alone.

At my lowest, I felt weak, disgusted with myself, and unable to endure another day. I saw no hope but kept crying out to God. I wondered why this was all happening. Had I done something wrong? Was this punishment? Would it ever be over? My kids didn't and still don't understand. My husband, God bless him, has stood by me when he had no idea how to help. At times, he'd want to cry or tell me to snap out of it, or he'd avoid talking to me altogether. He saw me fine one day, and in the pit the next.

My perception of God was altered. I cried out for help. I wondered if He was punishing me, had forgotten me, or was teaching me a lesson. I became angry with Him, and I didn't want to pull out my Bible because I felt it was not working. All this time, He never once snapped at me. He always spoke gently. Even when I couldn't feel Him, He never left me. Not once! Someone or something always showed up. Even my cat came to my rescue during many restless nights when I fell asleep in my prayer closet, where I felt safe. She'd come over to me, nuzzle me with her head, then curl into my side and sleep while I held her. My dogs also know when I need something.

The point is, Jesus loves me. He loves you. He doesn't want to leave us where we are in our messes. He was willing to take our sins and pay full price for them. No coupons necessary and no refunds, just love, paid in full.

Please, oh please, dear one, let Him in. Don't let pride or embarrassment keep you from crying out. I know it can feel like you're all alone and discounted, pun intended.

Worthless, broken, etc. I know how it feels to want to hide away in shame, guilt, and condemnation, but please don't.

Cry out to Him! Seek help! Scream, hit something like a pillow, or smash a plate. Reach out and do not remain silent in isolation, withering away. You are loved. God has chosen you, and His love does not have an expiration date.

The Crayon Box

Do you ever have one of those days when you just want to brush your teeth with Nutella? I know I sure do. This happens to be an oddity about myself that I adore. As a matter of fact, yesterday, I found myself making lunches for my sons, and they apparently didn't like what I was making them and felt led to share said opinions quite vigorously and with fervor.

My already semi-anxious mind flew straight to wanting to soothe my frazzled nerves with food. It just so happened to be that I targeted the open and very lusciously full jar of Nutella in front of me. I feverishly dunked my index finger into the chocolatey goodness and proceeded to rub my teeth with the delectable spread. I did this before my mind caught up with my wild emotions and wrangled those bad boys into submission, but not before my taste buds had a glorious yippee-ki-yay and hallelujah sugar rush moment.

Another quirk about me is that I also have an affinity for glitter that, despite my age, has not dissipated over time, regardless of the many gibes from my well-meaning middle sister, acquaintances, and co-workers, hubby, and friends. Okay so, a lot of people. I would have glitter in abundance in our home if I could. Glitter nails on my hands, glitter tiles on the floor, cups, shoes, clothes, glitter pet collars, and more! The more, the merrier. Some of my friends believe it to be a gangrenous infection. Once exposed to it, they will surely find it many moons later in the carpet, their clothes, their hair, and more, much to the detriment of their stalwart avoidance of all things that sparkle and shine. I'll convert them yet!

Who knew such pomp and circumstance could reside in such an itty-bitty speck of plastic and cause an uproar of ubiquitous objection! That's okay. I'll keep it to my fabulous self and ride on in joy and wonder. I'm the girl who loves to fake accents while talking to my kids and reading stories. My boys pretend to be irritated when they secretly adore my genuine goofiness and desire to laugh. I not only carry on like that at home but out in public. That's right, people, I'm that mom. You know, the one that much to the chagrin of her children and their enthusiastic eye-rolling, will embarrass, educate, and entertain them in front of gawking strangers even when they persist in begging me to stop in order to save their hides from red-cheeked mortification.

I lick the sauces off plates after I eat in restaurants, write and sing songs to my boys about our flatulent papillon, rhinos covered in cheese, and so much more. I'm also not afraid to talk to strangers and hug them, causing my kids to believe that I know the person. I talk about Jesus and the Bible all of the time, give strangers encouragement cards, cry in public, and make sure to read the Bible to my boys, pray over them, and sing.

I have not always had the guts to do that, but after all that I've been through and the importance of people knowing God loves them, it is worth the awkward jitters. My husband says we are polar opposite. I think in color, very vibrant, lively, passionate color, and he thinks in black and white. At one time, that made me feel deficient, rejected, and alone, but I'm not. God made me this way. I am colorful, effervescent, emotional, stubborn, and, dare I say, bold.

Now, onward fair and fellow companions to the squirrel moment leading into the meat of the chapter. When's the last time you went on a family vacation? On a scale of one to ten, how annoyed, vexed, perplexed, irritated, and generally sick of your fellow sojourners were you by the time you reached your intended destination? Was your spouse's favorite song annoyingly burned into your memory on a constant loop, searing it forever into your hippocampus?

Has your seat been kicked so many times from behind by your darling child, who you've already reminded for the umpteenth time not to do so because your back feels like a shattered pinata that no mastermind of a chiropractor could ever remedy? Half of the time, your climate control has been hijacked because your spouse prefers Antarctic cryogenic freezing temps on hurricane gale blasts, and you favor something more of a toasty warm wood-burning fireplace, but only on your feet. You must, of course, keep a gentle breeze of cooler temps outside on your face at all times at the very safe speed of Mach 5. Just kidding. Not really. Let's say about seventy to eighty miles per hour, sun, rain, or shine.

Road trip food is greasy, carb-saturated, and repetitive. Needless to say, bathroom breaks will be constant, painful, and perhaps legendary. If you have boys who just can't hold it any longer, a quarrel tends to ensue with your better half about how sanitary it would be to permit those little fellas to go number one into a recently consumed bottle of soda.

You've been wearing the same clothes and perhaps the same undergarments because you must break your journey at a hotel for the night. There is no way on God's green earth that you could possibly reach your suitcase, let alone survive the avalanche of everything your honey had packed, wedged, and shoved into submission into the back of your multi-passenger mini-van, tighter than any professional hoarder could ever dare to dream of.

Our floorboards are another story entirely. Mount Everest has got nothing on the piles we can accumulate! What treasures lie beneath? Who knows? Somewhere amidst the heap of discarded candy wrappers, neglected half-eaten chips, and crackers are empty cups of soda that have now reached an epoxy stage of adhesiveness that could rival any national brand. Why stop here on this tour of our seven-layer dip, so to speak. The excavation has merely begun! We still get to pass through the uncharted waters of broken crayons and misbehaving markers that seem to have miraculously lost their tops. Onward we go through the wilds of petrified fries that could double as lethal spears and rock-hard half-eaten chicken nuggets. Those babies could take an eye out if launched at an unsuspecting passenger.

Next are the jackets that supposedly do not exist in the winter and magically evade detection on a freezing winter's day, when your sweety swears before school that they have absolutely nothing to wear and cover their obviously freezing little bodies. A rare breed of stray sock emerges for a few precious seconds for air before being seized mercilessly and tugged back under the suffocating hubbub to regions yet unexplored, probably kidnapped by crystalized gummy bears, whose feet have become one with the mats. Perish the thought of interior fabric remaining clean. This mobile family circus has tested the boundaries of sanity, shed tears of joy, laughed until almost wetting themselves, and avoided another world war with timely played movies.

At last, this caravan reaches its final destination. Seatbelts fly off well before the van is in park. Bodies are tripped over as limbs fly and land undeserved punches to other flight members. The doors can't open fast enough to deliver this crew to solid ground. Forget proper exit procedure. It is every critter for themselves.

Children are barefoot, and parents are bloated, but no one seems to mind. We inhale the fresh air, crack our backs and knuckles, and smiles light up everyone's eyes again. We've finally made it! In one piece! No one is demented, and no one has tossed their cookies. Chuck did not even come up. Not once! Hallelujah! Praise dance in the parking lot!

You cannot believe how beautiful the resort is! As a matter of fact, someone in the family left the whole thing to you in their will. Palm trees sway in a gentle breeze. Sunlight glistens on top of pristine pool waters. The highest thread count linens await your tootsies on your ultra-mega California king-sized bed, while room service caters to your every whim.

Chocolate-covered strawberries from Belgium, no biggie. Macarons from France, of course! Little fish to polish off the callouses on your preciously worn-out feet? Done! We have a private gym with the latest equipment, superstar trainers, and meal shakes to satisfy every craving, clean your insides better than any flim-flam online fad and feed your brain, all while making your skin glow brighter than any freshly powdered baby's bottom you've ever seen.

You have a private airfield, top-notch world-famous chefs, privately designed clothes, and more. There's just one teensy weensy problem. Even though you've legally been given this fabulous resort, with anything you could ever desire is legally yours, it is locked up tighter than Fort Knox and Alcatraz have ever been. There are burly guards at the gate bearing arms of both kinds. You decide to walk in anyway but quickly find out you are most unwelcome. As a matter of fact, you get the feeling you might possibly be in danger. To be on the safe side, two of you stay while the rest of your family hightails it back to the safety of the van.

You have a distinct feeling that you are being watched. A fog begins to settle in a menacing manner as the two of you huddle together, waiting for hounds to be unleashed at any moment. No doubt they are highly trained with your scent already buried in their olfactory receptors, and they are malicious and possibly know martial arts. Just saying.

Your skin begins to crawl, your arm hair stands to attention, your legs wobble, making spaghetti proud, and sweat blinds you. But wait, what's that in the distance? A red light glows like a beacon, drawing you near like a moth to a flame. As you approach, a scantily-clad woman is pacing in the window. Hold the phone. This is not the resort I believed I had. This is most certainly not Amsterdam or Prague. She is absolutely staring you two down. Before you can protest, yelp, or run, she winks at you and bids you to come inside with her hand flagging you down.

The door creaks open, and your face flushes red as this woman dons a robe, signaling you to follow her. Up the stairs you go into a small, beautifully furnished kitchen. She asks you to take a seat at the table as she makes a pot of coffee and one of tea. She joins you, placing a steaming cup in your hand. She smiles and extends her hand to shake yours. You attempt to remain calm as you clasp her hand and tremble. She has a firmer grip than you thought possible for such a small woman.

Your bewildered faces bring a chuckle to her smiling lips. "Hi there, the name is Rahab. Pleased to meet ya! I heard about your family. I know you're the new owners. Stories about your great-grandpa have been told around these parts for years. To be honest, the boss here is none too pleased you've arrived and he's already sent his guards out to chase you down and handle his dirty work."

"But, if you'll promise me I can stay here when you move in and take over, then I'd be delighted to hide you two, just until the heat dies down of course. Don't want ya'll dying now, do we?"

Wait, what? This itty-bitty woman across from the two of you, aside from her minuscule attire, is savvy, kind, vivacious, caring, gracious, and direct. Come to think of it; you've never met someone so unexpectedly colorful. The entire situation still dumbfounds you as her charming country twang slips past her lips once more to add a stipulation. She'll hide you and help you escape if, and only if, you allow her and her family to stay once you've returned with your entire clan as backup to evict the slimeballs that run this place.

Her head tilts to the side, eyes suddenly serious as she asks if you have a deal. You only have a moment to decide before there is a loud and forceful banging on the front door. This time there is no hesitation. This place is your birthright, and you aren't leaving it to the lowlifes outside.

You nod your head in consent, and Rahab quickly brings you to an upper room that you've not noticed before, probably because you were too busy gawking at little Ms. Colorful. She silently shushes you and retreats back downstairs to answer the door.

"Well, hey there darlin, how ya doing?" Rahab begins to chatter faster than the angry voices at the door can keep up. She's as slick as a greased pig doing a 5K. There is no way that they will catch enough to slow her down. Their brains can't function past her sweet looks and honeyed words. A few more disgruntled groans and the door slams shut. Angry voices echo in the street and slowly fade away. Rahab climbs the stairs surprisingly fast for such a small thing. "It's safe, for now. I told those fellas you were long gone and if they hurried, they could catch ya!"

She didn't have to tell us twice. We took the hint. She showed us to the fire escape out of a back window reminding us all the while about our promise we made to allow her and her family to stay. As we hit the ground running, we could hear her faint country accent echoing in the night. "Ya'll come back now, ya hear?"

As farfetched as this sounds, it isn't that far from the truth of the Bible. Okay, the bare bones of the story are true, but the rest was my own fanciful imagination having a fiesta on its own. Lord, have mercy, that was fun!

In the book of Joshua, the Israelites, after wandering in the desert for forty years, an entire generation dying off, finally reach the promised land God gave them. There's one problem, a huge one. There are people already occupying it, so two men are sent as spies into the land. They decide to lodge with Rahab, a harlot. Not my words but true, nonetheless. Rahab and her people in Jericho already knew about the Israelites and their God, and they were terrified. The king of Jericho got wind of the two spies and sent men looking for them. Rahab hid the spies.

And as for her hiding them, she did indeed bargain with them for her life and those of her own family to be saved. What a woman! Colorful, indeed. A harlot, a protector, a liar, a clandestine purveyor of hiding spots for enemy spies, intelligent, persuasive, and, oh yeah, in the family line of not only King David, but Jesus.

Your mind might be going tilt right now if you've never heard of Rahab before. It seems unlikely that she became a savior of two spies and eventually in the family line of Jesus, but she did. Would you ever think of purposely using a crayon from your crayon box named Harlot? How about Liar? Sinner? What about a crayon named scam artist? I'm sure that would tickle your fancy. People may label you a strange name. They may dull your sparkle if you let them. You may bend and break under their scrutiny and rough usage, but sweetheart, even if you are despondent, even if you break, broken crayons still color.

As cliché as that sounds, it is so very true! 100%. Putting your broken pieces into the loving hands of our Father can only benefit you. He'll take your weirdness, your sorrows, your strengths, your glitter loving proclivities and shape and mold them into something so magnificent that the world will wait with bated breath to see you unveiled as a new crayon, wildly colorful, unmatched, and vitally necessary to brighten up the darkness in this world.

The Black Box

As a military spouse, I am well acquainted with the tragedies of planes going down and airmen losing their lives. Widows grieve, and the community is stunned. Names of those lost appear in military newspapers after the families have been contacted but not before the rumor mill has already begun between spouses and locals. You overhear whispers in the grocery stores, read speculation online, and hear from your neighbors the sad story relayed, only to find out that it was a senseless training accident. Families and friends gather along with the town to hold a vigil. Flowers are laid in front of photos. Candles flicker, and light dances across faces and shoulders huddled together in sniffling consolation as bodies quake.

What happened? Why did the plane go down? Was it mechanical? The weather? Was it sabotage or mutiny? As unlikely as that last one sounds, you never know. No, wait, that's not right. You can know exactly what went wrong. Every flight has something virtually indestructible that records each stinking malady underwent: A black box. This little golden nugget is a storehouse of information, like a nurse triaging you to take your vital signs before the doctor sees you. The nurse checks your temperature, weight, height, age, checks your pulse, blood oxygen level, and inquires after your symptoms and their duration of said disagreeable events. All of that information is stored to keep a record and provide the professional with a mental picture of the little foreign invaders wreaking havoc on your body, leading to a diagnosis about what you have, how you got it, and how to treat it. You leave with a printed-out record of this lovely visit to the E.R. and perhaps with a prescription or two or eight. You trudge past other nurses at the double door exit. They smile and share best wishes for healing, all while pushing a button that releases the doors from their locks. You leave the hospital into the fresh morning air, maybe with a limp, most likely under the influence of meds, and your printed report of what is wrong with you, a wristband with your name and date of birth, and a hopeful remedy.

A black box from a crash really is no different. You get initial diagnostics, and a picture comes to life. The pilots' conversations are on record, every single word. It records altitude, speed, fluid levels, malfunctions, and more. At some point of sifting through this holy mess of a tragedy, you shout, "Eureka!" You've found the hidden booger of a demon that infested the aircraft and caused it to crash. Now you have to decide what to do with the information. Do you allow it to fester inside of you, causing maladaptive rot to remain? Do you let anger fester and worm into your heart and mind and strangle you from the inside out?

Do we allow the senseless pain from our black box records to traumatize us into submitting our minds and hearts over to a sinister report? We can. We can cave. We can allow those slimy daggers to sink in, or we can realize that our black box contains records not only of the bad events but also the good. Sometimes I believe we hold on to past trauma and pain because it is all we seem to recognize anymore. We cling to dysfunctional illusions like a sick crutch because anything outside of the pain feels wrong. We've become blind. Our eyes glaze over, and we become numb, and hearts slowly harden into stone.

We clutch that black box like a gleaming trophy, like we are proud of it. We crave the attention we get when we tell a person about the contents of our box. We scrunch our brows together and relay the data, verbatim, until one day, the thrill of telling the story doesn't excite us so much anymore. The words don't ring so true, and we slowly begin to realize that there was good too, and we can choose to focus on the good. We choose joy. You, sweet darling, can choose joy.

You're probably thinking, "Now hold on there, you don't know what I've been through!" You may be right. I might not. But the answer to your problem and mine is the same. We have to give up our black boxes and choose to move on through the pain, the past, the memories, and fix our eyes on Jesus. It might sound trite, but I find that He truly is the answer to *every problem*.

In the book of Ruth, there is a woman named Naomi. Naomi, her husband, and their two sons had to uproot from their home in Bethlehem. If this were today, it would be like the nuts buying out most of the food and sanitary items from the stores and online due to the coronavirus, forcing you to uproot your family. Ideally, you'd go somewhere with food, healthcare, and plenty of toilet paper. Ha Ha Ha! I'm sorry, I had to. But I digress.

Naomi and her family moved to the heathen land of Moab. They remained there until a pivotal moment crept in. Elimelech, Naomi's hubby, passed away. I'm not sure why or how, and his death left her a widowed mother of two sons. At least she still had her sons to provide for her. Then her sons married.

Naomi became a mother-in-law to two women from Moab: Orpah and Ruth. Life went along, as it does, and they lived there about ten years before tragedy struck again. Mahlon and Chilion, her sons, died. There were no grandsons or granddaughters to speak of. I'm not sure how Naomi picked herself up off the floor and continued on, but she did.

She must have had such mental and emotional pain that it plagued her body too. Our minds are amazing and terrifying at the same time. I can only imagine the pressure she must have felt in her chest. Perhaps she clutched at it as she crumpled to the ground with her back against the wall and tears streaming down her blanched cheeks, creating a pool on the floor by her legs. She'd rock back and forth and let out sobs that would shatter the hearts of anyone within a thousand miles that could hear her crying out. Maybe Orpah and Ruth, with trembling hands and their own tear-streaked faces, knelt by Naomi and sobbed together until their eyes were swollen and dry.

They'd curl up next to each other in that corner and pass the night in a restless, discomforting sleep until the sun would rise. It always does. Light would spill into their dwelling place, across the floor, and eventually warm their feet as it crept up over their pain-ridden, stiff bodies. Their eyes would peel open in response to the light, and the women would breathe in the new day until the memory of yesterday would flatten them against the wall once more. But then they would begin to hear voices talking about a miracle. God had indeed given His people in Bethlehem bread again. Naomi's heart would flutter from a dead stillness into a fire. Hope would stir her to move. She would try to rise but find her limbs stiff and unwilling.

It would be then that Orpah and Ruth would glance at each other across their mother-in-law's head and nod slowly in agreement through bloodshot eyes. They would stand to their feet and simultaneously grasp Naomi's hands and arms and aid her to stand up. The rush of blood to Naomi's head would almost make her swoon, but Orpah and Ruth would have her firmly in hand. They wouldn't let her collapse again.

Naomi would politely but firmly signal the girls to release her, and she would go out into the sun and resolve to head back home. Orpah and Ruth would begin to follow Naomi, but she wouldn't have it. Her heart was so heavy and grieved. She would wish them farewell and pray God would give them rest and a new husband each. She'd kiss them good-bye in a bittersweet moment, and they'd weep. They wanted to go with her, but Naomi told them to turn back. The heart of hers would ache and begin to callous over from tragedy.

> But Naomi said, "Turn back, my daugh-ters; why will you go with me? Are there still sons in my womb, that they may be your husbands? "Turn back my daughters, go—for I am too old to have a husband. If I should say I have hope, if I should have a husband tonight and should also bear sons. Would you wait for them till they were grown? Would you restrain yourselves from having hus-bands? No, my daughters; for it grieves me very much for your sakes that the hand of the Lord has gone out against me!"
>
> Ruth 1:11–13 (NKJV)

I know this tactic. I know it too well. I know, and I'm sure many of you do too: Self-preservation by pushing away those that love you when you're in pain, even when you don't mean it. You feel like a caged animal with nowhere to go to escape the pressure, tearing at your skin, just to feel something other than utter despair and hopelessness. You project your inner turmoil onto others in hopes that they will back the heck up. Isn't it just like God to send someone to pursue you anyway with a love that mystifies you, unsettles you, and persists, no matter what rebuttal clings to your lips! Ruth would not back off following Naomi no matter the litany of excuses running like ticker tape through Naomi's mind.

> But Ruth said, "Entreat me not to leave you, or to turn back from following after you; For wherever you go, I will go: And wherever you lodge, I will lodge; your people shall be my people, and your God, my God. Where you die, I will die, and there will I be buried. The Lord do so to me and more also, if anything but death parts you and me."
>
> Ruth 1:16–17 (NKJV)

Ruth was a determined, loyal little thing. She was not backing down, and that, my darling, was love shining through the darkness, cracking open Naomi's impenetrable black box to reach its confines and begin bathing her heart with tenderness, easing her aches with a soothing balm of hope.

Yes, I am taking liberties here, but honestly, do you truly know how powerful love is? It wears down even the roughest heart with its gentle, steady waters and turns it into something smooth, receptive, and alive again. As Steve Urkel famously said in *Family Matters,* "I'm wearing you down baby, I'm wearing you dooooooown!" For those of you in your thirties or older, you know exactly what I'm talking about! It's funny to imagine God's love that way, but it sprang to mind, so it must have been the Holy Spirit. He has a sense of humor, just saying.

Naomi decided to stop speaking to Ruth. When they arrived in Bethlehem, there was a welcome party, so to speak. The whole city was excited to see them, wondering aloud if it was indeed Naomi back home. Ah, towns. Everyone knows everyone and their business and their momma's business, and their second cousin on their momma's side thrice removed and such. Naomi was not thrilled at their warm welcome. She even reinvented herself. She decided to give herself a new name, Mara. Mara means bitter. She was willing to replace her own sweet name with something destructive and self-deprecating because of her circumstances. It must have been a painful reminder of her former joy to be called Naomi. She blamed God for afflicting her and dealing bitterly with her. When we are so full of sourness, self-pity, and anger, our view of God becomes skewed. An inky blackness seeps in, threatening to smother the light and love right out of us, leaving an expressionless shell of our formerly vivacious selves.

Ruth and Naomi arrived at the beginning of the barley harvest. How fortunate and timely that they leave behind the old for the new. They were able to harvest what they did not sow. They will be able to reap because God is that good! He is gracious. He provides, even when we don't see it. Even when we think our world is upside down, and maybe it is.

You may fight His goodness because all you know and are willing to see is bad. But his ways and plans are so different from our own, even when He may lead us kicking and screaming and pounding His chest, perhaps swearing at Him.

Ruth went out to find work. Naomi approved. Ruth found a field where grain was being harvested. She followed behind the workers, gathering up what little leftovers they dropped behind. She must have been rather lovely because the owner of the field took notice of her and asked about who she was. He got the backstory of how Ruth had lost her husband, left everything, and cared for her mother-in-law, and it set his heart on fire with admiration. Boaz was his name. And guess what? He just so happened to be a relative on her deceased husband's side. So handsome, rich, godly, honorable, and kind, and he noticed Ruth. Wowza!

"The Lord repay your work, and a full reward be given you by the Lord God of Israel, under whose wings you have come for refuge" (Ruth 2:12, NKJV). This man then followed up what he said by feeding Ruth. He allowed her enough food until she was full and gave her extra to take home to Naomi. Glory to God! What a man! He offered her protection, kindness, food, and so much more. She must have trotted home with a skip in her step and rosy cheeks full of blush. No way would Naomi miss that! In fact, as soon as she found out whose field it was that Ruth had gleaned from, she got some pep in her step and began to praise God.

"Then Naomi said to her daughter-in-law, 'Blessed be he of the Lord, who has not forsaken His kindness to the living and the dead!' And Naomi said to her, '"his man is a relation of ours, one of our close relatives'" (Ruth 2:20, NKJV). From this point on, Naomi did a 180 and hatched a plan. She got a flipped script. Naomi saw a chance for redemption, and she took it! She instructed Ruth on how to approach Boaz in such a way as to honor him and save their family legacy through marriage.

There was a hitch in the plan, though. Boaz was not first in line to redeem the family, but in the presence of others, the first potential redeemer did not want to take on a new bride and lose his own legacy. Boaz indeed took Ruth as his bride and one might think this a fairy tale conclusion to a story laden with woe, but it was only the beginning.

> Boaz took Ruth and she became his wife; and when he went in to her, the Lord gave her conception, and she bore a son. Then the women said to Naomi, "Blessed be the Lord, who has not left you this day without a close relative; and may his name be famous in Israel! And may he be to you a restorer of life and a nourisher of your old age; for your daughter-in-law, who loves you, who is better to you than seven sons, has borne him.
>
> Ruth 4:13–15 (NKJV)

Naomi may have concluded that her life was irreparable, but God did not. In the deepest recesses of her heart, God kept the ember of hope aglow. He cranked up the heat, melted off the dross, intensified his love, even though she squirmed, and presented her as pure gold in the end. In all of this, He never left Naomi. He'll never leave you either.

So, you have a choice about that black box you've been carrying, clinging to desperation. You can choose only to see the record of wrongs and allow them to play over and over, wearing a groove into the "I'm a victim" vinyl. Or you can choose to see the good and drop that black box into the hands of Jesus and watch Him work, expect hope, and hold onto Him as He leads you into the unknown. Allow God to guide you when you don't know where you are going. When push comes to shove and you face dropping your crutch in order to embrace something new, you may feel like hurling and retreating into what's become your comforting dysfunction.

May I make a suggestion? Let go, baby doll. Step out anyway. Do it even when you feel afraid. Drop that black box and allow God to smash it with a hammer, a big God-sized hammer, and you shine, baby doll, you shine! Will it be scary? Yes. Will you scrounge around in the dark for a hand to grasp? Undoubtedly. Will your life ever look the same again? No. No, it will not, but that's okay. Keep your eyes on Jesus. Acknowledge your feelings, but tell them to shut up. Crucifying the flesh sucks. Excuse my word choice, please. The more you do it, the easier it gets, and the stronger you'll become. Focus on Jesus! Find out what He says about you. Find the truth in His word. Find out what He says about who He is and believe it.

Saturate yourself in that stuff until it oozes out of you like molasses: slow, strong, and sweet. That'll smother out the crud you held onto before in that black box. It really will. And then, my darling, walk on. That's right: One step at a time. Don't stress yourself out with grand schemes. Just keep walking. Be present in the moments. Take joy in your current situation. Play with your kids, enjoy that husband of yours, sit in the sun, and listen to the birds chirping. Be thankful on purpose. Before you know it, the crash that your box recorded will seem like a distant memory, and you won't even recognize the beauty you've become. What you see as impossible is indeed possible with God. Just don't leave Him out of the mix.

The Shoebox

In my closet, nestled together in a cubby of sorts, are two shoeboxes containing some of the most exciting, flashy, and expensive shoes that I have ever had the privilege to own. One pair is covered in glitter and crystals, probably rhinestones, but beautifully stunning to me. They are white and have a cross with wings on them. Gaudy to some, but girl, to me, breathtaking, particularly in the sunlight!

The second pair of boots are polar opposite in looks but just as spectacular! They are embellished with black sequins and crystals. I call them my Princess of the Night-Time Sky boots. No joke. Ask my husband, and he'll tell you. I will not tell you the price of these boots because you'd probably scold me for such a frivolous expenditure, but that wouldn't change my mind about them one bit! I remember having to break these suckers in. Oh, my bunions! That hurt! I wore my husband's thick military-issued winter socks. My feet hurt so much, but I was absolutely determined to wear them out and about. They needed to be stretched in order to fit better: the things we do for beauty and attention.

The thing is, as much as I want to wear them now, if I do, they cause pain, and I am totally aware that they will, and I wear them anyway. Sadly, I haven't taken those babies out for a day in the sun for quite some time now. Last summer, when I began breaking down emotionally and had cut out caffeine, I was exercising and rolled my ankle twice. Pain followed, of course, not for just a few days but almost a year now. I've been to my doctor on base, who happens to look like Doc from Back to the Future, had an x-ray, an MRI, and visited a podiatrist, but with little relief.

Back in November, we decided to go out shopping on Black Friday. The store was more packed than I could have possibly imagined. At one point, I was trying to push my cart to meet up with my husband and our kids when suddenly, someone behind me slammed into my Achilles tendon with their cart. They hit the same injured foot. I looked down to find the skin had been ripped off, and I was bleeding into my sock. Not long after this event, I woke up one morning to find fresh claw marks down the side of, you guessed it, the same foot.

My podiatrist gave me arch supports, but they didn't work. I kept having to go back to have the inserts readjusted. Another MRI was ordered with contrast. I am not a fan of having injections done. The first vein she did, didn't go well. The needle ended up blowing my vein, and my arm began to burn. It was unbearable! From my wrist to my shoulder, my arm felt like it was on fire. The kind lady assisting me put an icepack on my arm, and then did the injection on the other arm. Thankfully, that one worked!

Two weeks later, I got my MRI results back. According to the report and my doctor, I have mild plantar fasciitis, mild arthritic changes midfoot, heel spurs, bunions, and a little tear in my Achilles tendon. Apparently, I also have tight hamstrings and calf muscles and an extra bone in my foot. My doctor was quite fascinated but hopeful. Oh, and one leg is just a tad longer than the other. He was gleeful, actually. He said all of my problems were mechanical. I just needed the right support for my arches.

Since then, I have not worn my fantastic, sparkly, life-changing boots. I've had to leave them on the shelf while I turn to more practical footwear, my tennis shoes. My husband says it seems like I live in gym shoes and athletic clothes. That is mostly true. I spend most of my day in workout clothes and my tennis shoes because I am busy with my boys, exercise, housework, walking the dogs, and more. In that respect, my sneakers serve me well.

Funny how I long to hide my shyness or a lousy day behind something beautiful, but that beautiful thing causes me pain. I desire them because I believe they make me feel bolder than I am at times. The dazzling glitter reflecting the sun's light makes me feel more beautiful and special, boosting my confidence and stuffing my insecurities behind those sequins and rhinestones. If I want to heal, I have to put on drastically more comfortable shoes with stiff arch support and lackluster adornments. Don't get me wrong, I love my tennis shoes, but sometimes I want the glamour of my eye-catching, head-turning, expensive as all get out, sunshine encrusted boots of happiness. They really are all that and a bag of chips.

Last summer, I was on a walk around my neighborhood on the phone with a good friend, offering up good, sound Christian advice. Oh, I knew all the right things to say. I sounded very spiritual indeed. I knew the verses, had the right upbeat tone of voice, the right everything really, but there was a hollowness to it all. Once again, I'd brought sage advice and a superhero cape to a situation that I had not mastered in my own life. And that is when it happened. Right after the phone call ended, God said, "It's time to walk out your faith." In a manner that He seems to like, God dropped something into my spirit when I wasn't expecting anything other than feeling like a good Samaritan, wanting a trophy and a pat on the head.

I had no idea then what He meant, but I was about to learn firsthand. It was time to put my money where my mouth was, put the pedal to the metal, and walk in someone else's shoes. The only problem is when you don't know where you are going, you don't know what to wear. You have no idea what kind of shoes are required. You are blindsided, wearing a pair of shoes that you can't fit, feel, or even see, but somehow, you know they were made for you. You're about to begin a journey into the unknown that will require every bit of gumption and spiritual arsenal you have strapped onto your tootsies to face God knows what. And that's the thing: He knows! He knows, and no amount of panic on your part can come up with answers for where you're going. You can't grab sparkly boots to display confidence. No flip-flops will lighten up the mood. No gumboots will protect you from puddles, and no heels that make your legs go from here to heaven will ever prepare you for what's to come.

You are at once as terrified as you are excited. Fear grips you just as faith burns in opposition. Suddenly, you can't feel your legs because they are trembling violently as if the bottom has dropped out beneath you. Everything becomes dark, and you can feel panic creeping up your body, threatening to overtake you and pull you down into despair, but then a voice rings out in the darkness, and all it says is, "Come." You don't know why you feel compelled to move forward except that the voice is so comforting and rises just above the dark clouds accumulating above you. You're shaking as you look down at your bare feet.

Somehow, someway, a force within you urges you to take a step. "But nothing is there to catch you!" your mind shrieks. "You'll fall! And then what? You'll crash and burn and you won't recover! Do not take that step!" Wow. That doesn't sound right. Not one bit! You decided to tell the voice to shut up and raise your shaking foot to take a step. And wonder of wonders, when your foot lands, it lands on something solid. You take a glance down while holding your breath and something catches your eye. A pinprick of light begins to shine. Minuscule at first, it begins to snake up and over your foot, like a glimmering golden thread.

It travels beyond your foot and, before your very eyes, begins to form stitches in the darkness. The stitches begin to bind together, and the strap of a sandal starts forming. The light is dazzling, like nothing you've ever seen before! Courage begins to well up inside of you, bringing back feeling into your legs, and you take another step. The same thing happens again. The light begins to pulse and shine, and a strap materializes bit by bit on your foot.

You take another step, and then another, and another. Another strap molds itself so firmly but tenderly to your foot and the other. A heel and arch start lifting your feet up into perfect form, and now your excitement begins to make your heart race. Not only are these shoes fabricating themselves, but they are expelling the darkness as you go, bit by bit. You look again at your feet and notice how the golden threads seem to be quivering and alive, moving, revolving, energized, and purposeful. You kneel down to take a closer look and notice something that quickens your heartbeat and dilates your pupils. The light is fervent, determined, and unrelenting. It isn't actually threads that you see, but millions of letters running past your eyes at dizzying speeds, and yet you can still read it. The letters begin forming words, words you recognize, words of hope, faith, and love, courage, and undeniable truth.

Jeremiah 29:11 flashes by in a nanosecond. "For I know the plans I have for you," says the Lord, "plans to prosper you and not to harm you, plans to give you a hope and a future."

Then comes Romans 8:28, "And we know that in all things God works for the good of those who love Him, who have been called according to his purpose."

Following this is Isaiah 41:10, "So do not fear, for I am with you; do not be dismayed, for I am your God. I will strengthen you and help you; I will uphold you with my righteous right hand."

Then 2 Timothy 1:7, "For God has not given us a spirit of fear, but of power and of love and of a sound mind."

And on and on these words go, each step producing more and more light, and more and more of God's word swirls around your feet in golden wonder and forms glorious shoes out of thin air. You begin to realize that there, in the darkness, you are literally walking on the word of God. It is holding you up, even when you can't see where you are going. Tears begin to stream down your face as you take step after step. The light becomes brighter and brighter as the most unimaginably exquisite shoes continue to form, and then you notice something in your periphery. Tiny whispers spark in the darkness, evoking a discomforting feeling of dread as they shift into slithering words, oozing out of the inky void surrounding you. A chill races up your spine as the whispers multiply into millions of vicious and accusing taunts.

"How dare you think you can walk out your faith, you've done too much bad to deserve such goodness and light. You're a nobody. You'll never make it. Nothing will ever change! You're nothing. You're worthless. The nerve!"

The jibes continue, and your feet begin to falter. You feel like you're suffocating. Your heart races and skips what seems like a trillion beats. A cold sweat breaks out on your skin, and a shroud of darkness begins to lower on top of you, and you sink.

You sink slowly at first, but then you plunge into the abyss. Your arms reach far above your head in hopes of rescue. You scream out with lungs on fire, "Help!" before you are completely submerged. It is then that a hand full of light and strength clasps your arm, and you rise to the surface. Surprisingly, the taunts, the lies, the darkness are all still around you, but you do not pay them any attention.

You take a chance and look down to find the shoes are still brightly shining on your feet. A pair of hands firmly grasp your face, gently raising your gaze to meet the kindest pair of eyes you have ever seen. A peace rushes through your body like a warm blanket wrapping you in a hug, and somehow you know you'll be all right. Is the onslaught of terrifying words still swirling around? Yes. Is God's word still secure around your feet? Yes it is.

Are you still in the throes of a storm? Absolutely! But and I say but, your footing is secure in the one who spoke life over you. Scared and all, you are not alone.

In Matthew 14:22–33, Jesus insists on the disciples getting into their boat and sailing across the lake to the other side while he sent a large crowd home. Jesus went into the hills to pray by himself until nightfall. Meanwhile, the disciples were in a pickle. Their boat was way too far from land, and a storm had arisen. They were battling strong winds and heavy waves. In their eyes, there was no way anyone could reach them and help. Then around three in the morning, a figure came toward them. I was sure they didn't know whether to be freaked out by the storm or the ghostly apparition of a man walking on water toward them. I probably would have hurled on the deck by then and made uncontrollable laps on deck until I face-planted into a mast or another person, knocking myself out cold.

In their fear, the disciples screamed out that it was a ghost, but it wasn't. It was Jesus, out for a stroll on the waves, wind whipping around him, peace as a garment, and authority in his gaze.

The storm rages on, and the boat is still rocking, probably taking on water, and Jesus basically says to chill out; it's him. I'm not sure what got a hold of Peter, but he decided to ask Jesus to invite him to get out of the boat in the storm, mind you, and come walking to the Prince of Peace on the water, possibly with fish smacking him in the face. Jesus said to come, so Peter did! I've heard of waterproof shoes before, but not this waterproof! Peter did indeed walk on the waves to Jesus until he looked away and fear crept in. He began to sink and cried out to Jesus to save him, and he did!

He cried out and immediately reached out and grabbed him. He asked Peter why he had such little faith. At this point, many people judge Peter for flipping out and sinking. But how many people do you know other than Jesus and him that have walked on water?

The thing that I noticed was that when Peter cried out, Jesus immediately grabbed hold of him and pulled him up to safety because, in case you missed it, the storm still raged on. He either teleported across the water to Peter instantaneously or like a cheetah running across water or, he was right there already, and Peter still sank. They walked back to the boat together, still in the wind and the waves, but together. They climbed aboard, and the storm ceased. What faith Peter must have had to walk on the waves. He walked on the word of God to the Word of God. Now how do you ever prepare to take steps like that? Would you have donned those kinds of shoes and stepped out in faith to get to your savior, or would you have looked down at your fresh new kicks, whatever they may be, and turned back, feeling fear, shame, inadequacy, comparison, and more?

It is all fun and games until God literally says it is time to walk out your faith, and you are faced with a screaming storm with no shoes, but your savior calls from a distance and says, "Come." My sparkly boots and orthopedic shoe inserts in my sneakers could never allow me to walk the walk that God called me out to. Neither can your shoes, but your faith, as small or large as may be, will activate the footwear to form when you heed your Maker's call and step out. This is no small feat, and I applaud you most vigorously! Take one step, and then another, and another. Wait on God. Choose his word over the trash in life, even your own feelings and thoughts, and keep moving. Do not quit.

> "So put on all the armor that God gives you. Then when the evil day comes, you will be able to defend yourself, And when the battle is over, you will still be standing firm" (Ephesians 6:13, ESV).

The Toolbox

Three days ago, I sat for two to three hours on my couch, barefoot and sanding off callouses with a rotary pedicure tool I'd purchased recently. My feet have been rough for quite some time, and because of the widespread Covid-19 virus, everyone has pretty much been housebound, which means no pedicures at the spa; a first-world problem for sure, but a problem nonetheless. The ball of my foot had so much callous on the side, behind my big toe, and on my heel that I seemed to be developing hooves. I'd pick at the skin until the cracks became jagged shards and sometimes open tears, creating very tender, inflamed, and ugly sores. So, I busted out my rotary pedicure tool and had a go.

The smoother grit attachment did not work! It barely tickled and certainly did not have the effect of what I needed. What I needed was much rougher in order to tackle the damage I'd done to my feet. To take down the wear and tear I'd built up by walking barefoot outside in my driveway on concrete, sometimes on the road when I'd get the mail, at other times, pacing the house out of boredom or checking on all of the locks and lights before bed. I had hardened up my soles over time, and it was going to take something drastic to undo the damage that I had actually built up to protect my feet. That protection, however, had become unsightly and at times painful while accumulating.

So, to remedy that, I got out my pedicure tools, plopped onto my couch, flicked on the TV, and powered up the sander. I watched my dead and dry skin collect in the tool's cradle beneath the sanding bit as the rest blew away into the surrounding atmosphere, and often, into my face. At first, it was amusing. My couch, my lap, and my tools were all finely dusted with, well, me. Dead parts of me were obliterated into a fine powder. It kind of seemed like chalk or when you go to an Italian restaurant, and the waiter grates parmesan onto your pasta, but finer and more abundant. Then my mind ran to the reality that I was created from the dust of the earth, and to dust, my body will return: Kind of morbid and awe-inspiring at the same time.

The sanding continued; my skin dust still flew and powdered the surrounding area while I waited, and waited, and waited. I knew my feet were rough, but good grief, I didn't realize just how long it would take for my feet to be smooth as a baby's bottom. I had even contemplated busting out my husband's Dremel tool from the garage. Oh yes, I sure would have used it! Only the thought of it being dirty made me pause.

Yes, my feet were rough. Yes, they were in dire need of some attention, but was I willing to use a tool on myself that could possibly inflict more pain and result in something putrid and infectious? Or would I go the sanitary route with something clean, pure, radiant, and unused to chisel down my roughened edges and resurrect something hopeful, something precious, and something new? I'm not crazy. Option B it is! No chance of gangrenous tootsies for this gal! Both paths and tools could be painful. Chipping away and stripping away layers of yourself is never fun. It is not a weekend DIY project found online with a complete list of tools and instructions at the ready. It is an arduous task that can often take months or years to tear down and rebuild, but it is totally worth it! I promise you! When you have things built up inside of you, from who knows what, and for who knows how long, a stronghold is constructed in your heart and mind, a dark tower if you will.

Often, it is a result of self-protection because things were inflicted upon you by others, and you were harmed and not able to resist building up your wall, stone by stone, around your heart. All it takes is one stone, then another, and another, and another. Pretty soon, you've got yourself an assembly line coming your way on a conveyor belt. This one says, "You're ugly!" The next says, "You're a loser." Then, "You aren't smart enough. My ex was better than you. You're a terrible mom. Why can't you keep the house clean? You're too fat."

"You're too skinny. You will never make enough money. Other people get their prayers answered, but not yours. Pathetic. Useless. Waste of talent. Sterile. Jobless. Broke. Too sick. Don't even bother getting up. Just stay down."

The stones keep coming, and you keep taking them. One by one, you build a wall around yourself. You slap on some mortar, and the darkness begins to creep in. All this time, you were trying to keep it out to build up defenses, an impenetrable fortress, but the opposite occurred. You've walled yourself in with no way out, and now, you can only wait.

The silence is actually quite deafening until you begin to hear the same ugly words as before, and you panic. How are they inside with you? How are they echoing around you? How are they circling your entire being with such malicious ferocity? Who is saying these horrible things? And then you realize the words were no longer outside but were now pouring forth from your own lips, burying you and any tools that might have helped you escape.

Sounds pretty desolate, right? Sounds like no escape, yes? What if I told you, you are wrong in this assumption, that there is a way of escape, and the tools you need have been with you all along. Would you jump at the chance to find them? Would you scramble on your hands and knees in the dark until your fingertips brushed across something strong, something different, something with a glimmer of hope and light? Would you take hold of the tool with a fresh determination? I know I would. I'd grab hold of that thing and never let go!

In the book of Acts, Paul and Silas were on their way to prayer and met a female slave who had a demon spirit that allowed her to predict the future. She made a whole lot of money for her owners by fortune-telling. For some reason, she began following the men, shouting after them for many days. I imagine my nerves would have been shot, hearing her over and over, kind of like my kids during this lockdown because of Covid-19. They, however, shout very different things than the woman in the story. They tell me how much they hate me. They yell, pitch fits, give me ugly looks, and even hiss. They are sealed with the Holy Spirit and not demon-possessed, but their words can feel that way to me sometimes.

Words are a tool that can tear down, build up, create something new, destroy, soothe, anger, poison, wound, frighten, heal, set free, and love. The words you hear and say can do these things. The question is, what will you believe, and what will you do with these words? The girl followed these men.

She followed Paul and the rest of us,
shouting, "These men are servants of

124

the most High God, who are telling you
the way to be saved." She kept us up
for many days. Finally Paul became so
annoyed that he turned around and said
to the spirit, "In the name of Jesus Christ
I command you to come out of her!" At
that moment the spirit left her.

Acts 16:17-18

In my mind, I am ecstatic that the torment and bond-
age plaguing this girl ended at the name of Jesus Christ! If she
were my daughter, and I heard those words from Paul and
witnessed her emancipation, I would have run to my girl,
gathered up her limp body, and wept with joy as I watched
the light and life return to her eyes. I would smile and rock
her back and forth, her arms wrapped around my waist,
knowing she was safe and healed. We'd share this truth with
grins turned toward each other and then towards Paul and
Silas. Our gaze would fall on the crowd that we'd forgotten
around us, and our mouths would falter at their brutal and
perplexing visages. The enraged slave owners grabbed hold of
Paul and Silas, seized them actually, and dragged them off to
face the local authorities because they realized they had just
lost their hope of making money through the girl. "They
brought them before the magistrates and said, 'These men
are Jews, and are throwing our city into an uproar by advo-
cating customs unlawful for us Romans to accept or practice'" (Acts 16:20–21).

After the accusations were, the multitude witnessing
the event had an all-out fit! They rose up against Paul and
Silas, and the magistrates tore off their clothes and had them
beaten with rods and thrown into prison.

The magistrates put Paul and Silas into the inner prison and placed them in stocks. They earned this brutal treatment for an act of such love and kindness. How different the Romans' hearts must have been, prizing making money off of that poor, demon-possessed girl. God got the glory anyway through unusual and brutal circumstances, and His tools achieved it. A declaration from the demonic spirit led Paul to use the name of Jesus to cast it out and free the girl.

My mind would not have done so well. I know what a prison of words can do. I've experienced enough mental and emotional depravation, depression, and anxiety to know it is not a cushy place to set up camp and stay. I know how hard it is to sing praises to God when you feel so broken and can barely utter a word, but you must! You absolutely must!

Paul and Silas did. "About midnight Paul and Silas were praying and singing hymns to God, and the prisoners were listening to them" (Acts 16:25). Can you picture that? Paul and Silas, stripped, beaten, and imprisoned, but praying and singing hymns to God. And the prisoners were listening to them! You never know whom you are influencing in your current situation while using the Word of God as your tool.

While I was thinking about this, God reminded me that He inhabits His people's praises. He lives in them! My goodness! Can you just imagine this? Paul and Silas, praying and praising God, singing to Him as He literally lives in their words, creating an ongoing flow of God to Himself and through Himself, out of the mouths of Paul and Silas. Can you envision how charged the atmosphere must have been? The men were conduits of the Word, vessels of praise. "Suddenly there was a great earthquake, so that the foundations of the prisons were shaken; immediately all the doors were opened and everyone's chains were loosed" (Acts 16:26, NKJV).

My God, the beauty and terrifying freedom this moment must have been. While Paul and Silas were unjustly imprisoned, the others there listening, I'm reckoning, were actually deserving of being in jail, and yet the Word inhabiting Paul and Silas's songs, prayers, and praises fell on them too, setting them free. That makes me want to cry! The jailer awoke and panicked when he saw the prison doors. His mind went wild with assumptions that they had escaped, so he drew his sword to end his own life. I'm sure the devil would have loved that. God had a different plan. One that involved saving many lives.

Before the guard could take his own life, Paul shouted from the darkness for the guard not to harm himself and that all of the prisoners were still there. Such integrity! The guard lit a torch and came to Paul and Silas and fell to his knees, asking what he must do to be saved. Paul and Silas told the guard about Jesus Christ, our Lord. They spoke to the guard and then all who were in the guard's house, and they all believed in Jesus and were saved. He even washed their wounds, fed them, and then rejoiced with them because he and his household believed in God.

Paul and Silas were released the next day. They were Roman citizens, and that fact was unknown until the morning after their imprisonment. This tidbit of information made the magistrates very afraid. They went to the house of a woman named Lydia, shared encouragement with their brethren, then departed.

Words are very catching. They are tools that, when manifested, can build a person up, repair them, or tear them down. The question is, which way will you use this tool? Our thoughts, our words, literally change our brain's neural pathways. Depending on the words you've received, you may be free and basking in the glory of God because of who He says you are or, if you've taken to heart the negative words, the tool of the enemy, and buried behind a false wall. But God. That's what I've got to say. He flat out tells us how to change.

> Do not conform to the pattern of this world, but be transformed by the renewing of your mind. Then you will be able to test and approve what God's will is-his good pleasing and perfect will.
>
> Romans 12:2

> So then faith comes by hearing, and hearing by the word of God
>
> Romans 10:17 (NKJV)

> Now we ask you, brothers and sisters, to acknowledge those who work hard among you, who care for you in the Lord and who admonish you. Hold them in the highest regard in love because of their work. Live in peace with each other. And we urge you, brothers and sisters, warn those who are idle and disruptive, encourage the disheartened, help the weak, be patient with everyone. Make sure that nobody pays back wrong for wrong, but always strive to do what is good for each other and for everyone else. Rejoice always, pray continually, give thanks in all circumstances; for this is God's will for you in Christ Jesus. Do not quench the Spirit! Do not treat prophecies with contempt but test them all: hold on to

what is good, reject every kind of evil. May God himself, the God of peace, sanctify you through and through. May your whole spirit, soul and body be kept blameless at the coming of our Lord Jesus Christ. The one who calls you is faithful, and he will do it.

1 Thessalonians 5:12–24

Death and life are in the power of the tongue: and they that love it shall eat the fruit thereof.

Proverbs 18:21 (NKJV)

On that day David first delivered this psalm into this hand of Asaph and his brethren, to thank the Lord: Oh, give thanks to the Lord! Call upon His name: Make Known His deeds among the peoples! Sing to Him, sing psalms to Him; talk of all His wondrous works! Glory in His holy name; Let the hearts of those rejoice who seek the Lord! Seek the Lord and His strength; Seek His face evermore! Remember His marvelous works which He has done, His wonders and the judgments of His mouth, O seed of Israel His servant, you children of Jacob, His chosen ones!

1 Chronicles 16:7–13 (NKJV)

Let all bitterness, wrath, anger, clamor, and evil speaking be put away from you, with all malice. And Be kind to one another, tenderhearted, forgiving one another, even as God in Christ forgave you.

Ephesians 4:31–32 (NKJV)

I realize this may seem like a lot to take in, and there are many more verses like these, but they are a necessary tool. In my own home, I have to seriously do what the Word says in order to heal, transform, and just get through the day. It is essential in tearing down strongholds in my mind that have held preeminence for too long. I have to dig deep for the truth God says about me, others, and circumstances and speak that truth out loud until the blinders are off my eyes and God's healing balm flows through me and into the world. His word is kind of like a spiritual plunger. Sorry for the crude image, but sometimes we are so clogged, if you will, with years of wrong thinking, speaking, and doing; time to flush that crap out of our systems.

Proverbs 23:7 (NKJV) states, "For as he thinks in his heart, so is he."

This really is true. You may be thinking things that are just not true, so then, you speak it, think on it, act on it, and it becomes a reality to you, an altered and twisted reality, but a reality nonetheless. If, like me, you've experienced panic attacks and depression, then you know you could be in a situation where there is no danger at all, but your thoughts and words produce a danger reaction in your body, and things get wonky.

That's the nice way to put it. I know it doesn't feel that way, not in the least bit, but you get my drift.

When the kindness of God breaks through the anger, fear, insecurities, and depression, a change happens. The stones you erected begin to shake. A gentle word comes from a friend. A song on the radio speaks to your heart when you're driving alone and furious. You overhear a stranger say exactly what you needed to hear, and you find that wall crumbling a bit more, and light begins to shine into the darkness. That familiar ache dulls a bit, and you find the courage to pick up a tool and free yourself.

Go through the word of God, no joke. See what He has to say about you and your situation, and then, sweet girl, you begin speaking it out loud over yourself. I'm not kidding! Dig in your heels, find the truth and declare it! You will find with each passing day that the stones break even more as the word of God penetrates your heart, cradles it, and sings over it. That's right, He sings over you.

> "The Lord your God in your midst, The Mighty One, will save; He will rejoice over you with gladness; He will quiet you with His love, He will rejoice over you with singing" (Zephaniah 3:17, NKJV).

Be kind to yourself. Please. I beg of you! Speak God's truth over yourself. Many times, the problem takes time to go away because it took a while to build up. If you have a bad moment, day, or year, whatever, stop and remind yourself that it is okay. Track those internal lies, whip out your tools, and blast them to kingdom come, or file them down, one by one.

I have to take my own advice too. Don't think you have to be perfect either; that will drive you bonkers. You can drop that load off of your back right now. Even if your hands shake, take a deep breath, pick up your tool, and have at it!

Jack-in-the-Box

When I was little, there was a toy I had that was quite popular. It was a metal box with a brightly painted exterior displaying child-friendly circus clowns on all sides in bold primary colors. Reds, yellows, and blues danced around the edges and captured my attention with such delight inspiring contagious smiles. However, this was nothing compared to what lay inside. On top of the box was a lid or hatch, if you will. It was being held closed on the inside, containing a spring-loaded clown that would be released after you cranked the handle on the side repeatedly. I would shake in anticipation while I turned that crank over to a familiar song most kids my age would have known: "Pop goes the weasel." A very appropriate choice to accompany the rising tension. The thing is, I was the one cranking the handle. I knew exactly what lay dormant inside, waiting to emerge and startle the crud out of me, and yet, I persisted. You see, I knew exactly what was waiting in the darkness. I knew how to get it out. I knew the shock I'd receive. Heart palpitations would be followed by laughter, but, I didn't know exactly when the little critter would burst through the trap door and lunge at me.

I knew all of this, and I did it anyway. I'd shove that tightly coiled spring of a clown back into the hole from whence it came, with one hand, I might add, while closing the hatch down over its head with the other, forcing its presence back down into the dark recesses it came from. And then I would do it all over again. Why would I do that? Why would I bury something that only brought misery mixed with joy only to free it of my own volition?

It's kind of like emotions. You can bury those suckers to the point that they are no longer bothering you on the surface, but life gets in the way, as it does, and you resurrect those clowns by increasing the tension inside. Life gets a hold of the handle and vigorously cranks until pop goes the weasel.

So you stuff your emotions, pray they stay put and then crank the handle. You hear the music announcing the impending moment of doom, and whammo, out they come, uglier and more energetic than before. Now what? Do we keep on shoving down, sealing, burying, cranking, and exploding, only to repeat? Often, we go through so many rounds of surprise attacks and still think that slamming down the hatch will fix the situation, but it won't. Inevitably, what went down will come up with more and more ferocity until you've decided that you've had enough and you just let it all out. You can even become addicted to your self-inflicted victimhood. I've been there. I didn't like the prison bars. Jailbird was not, and never will be my name. God called me to freedom, and if I want to claim everything He said is already mine, then I'm going to have to purposely allow the jack-in-the-box out so I can break its hold on me.

What about when love comes springing out at you? Does it startle you? Does it seem real? Does it smack of cynicism and unbelief because you've been mistreated for so long? Is it hard to receive? Do you hunger after it but desire to shove it back into the box before you have to face the truth that you are loved and wanted? Not only does it leap out at you, but it draws you out from your reservations and into hope. Some people may not find this difficult at all. Some throw themselves at love like a starving dog on a T-bone, but others run for the hills as fast as their legs can carry them because the idea of being loved despite your flaws, failures, quirks, bad behaviors, and sins, just feels utterly wrong and impossible.

In the book of John, after going to Mount of Olives one morning, Jesus went into the temple, and all of the people came to him. I imagine it was packed! He sat down to teach them, but while he was teaching, the scribes and Pharisees brought a woman. These were men who knew the law! They wanted to trap Jesus to prove he wasn't who he said he was. The woman they brought, they set her right in the midst of everyone before speaking and calling out her sin publicly. She had been caught in the act of adultery. Lord only knows the state of dress she was in, or the lack thereof…, but there she was, on blast, in the middle of the teaching in the temple. I can imagine the shame she felt at being exposed like this so maliciously, not only to address her sin but to be used as a pawn in an attempt to discredit Jesus as the Messiah.

Had the scribes and Pharisees set a trap to catch her in the act? Did they have no shame for their actions? I can sit here pointing fingers at them self-righteously, but I am no better. None of us are. We've all been guilty of this in some way. Matthew 5:44 says, "But I say to you, love your enemies, bless those who curse you, do good to those who hate you, and pray for those who spitefully use you and persecute you."

She could be stoned to death as her punishment. Her heart probably beat against her ribs so ferociously she feared it would escape the confines of her body and fall to the ground, dying a death of mortification. Her ears probably barely registered the cold and calculated words of the scribes and Pharisees as she stayed put, frozen in fear, words dripping with disdain, aimed daggers at her while addressing Jesus in this poignant moment. "They said to Him, 'Teacher, this woman was caught in adultery, in the very act. Now Moses, in the law, commanded us that such should be stoned. But what do you say?'" (John 8:4–5, NKJV).

How thick do you think the tension was in there? Just hand out the knives because you could slice up that atmosphere and serve it with a side of crow in a moment. Jesus' validity was in question. They challenged if he knew the law or not. They baited him, or at least they thought they did. Smug little boogers. Jesus did not reply but instead stooped to the ground and began writing on it with his finger. Boy, would I love to know just where he was while stooped down and writing. The scribes persisted in the henpecking of Jesus with the same question until he raised himself to answer them. I wonder how close he was to the woman when he had stooped down. Did he catch her eye and smile in assurance or sympathy? Did his proximity and presence emanate so much that she could feel it? Did it quell her fears? Maybe her frightened heart rate slowed a beat or two. Maybe her hands slowed in their shaking.

The scribes and Pharisees kept pestering. They were incessant, kind of like my boys when they want something, pushing for a yes to their request. Jesus didn't break at their bombardment. "So when they continued asking Him, He raised Himself and said to them, 'He who is without sin among you, let him throw a stone at her first.' And again He stooped down and wrote on the ground" (John 8:7–8, NKJV).

I have no idea what he wrote, but perhaps he allowed the men time to mull over their thoughts and actions before they put their foot in it again. And just like that, the sound of stones plummeting to the ground began to shake the atmosphere. So the rocks cried out, so to speak, testifying to the fact that only Jesus was without sin and had the right to throw a stone at this woman. And he chose not to.

> When Jesus had raised Himself up and
> saw no one but the woman, He said to
> her, "Woman, where are those accusers of
> yours? Has no one condemned you?" She
> said, "No one, Lord." And Jesus said to
> her, "Neither do I condemn you; go and
> sin no more."
>
> John 8:10–11 (NKJV)

Wow! I mean, wow! Pop! Surprise! The jack is out of the box, and it is facing love. Those ugly things that popped up over and over are now in the light and exposed, and your Maker is not scolding you but setting you free through the exposure.

> Then Jesus spoke to them again, saying,
> "I am the light of the world! He who fol-
> lows Me shall never walk in darkness, but
> have the light of life
>
> John 8:12 (NKJV)

> For all that is secret will eventually be
> brought into the open, and everything
> that is concealed will be brought to light
> and made known to all.
>
> Luke 8:17 (NLT)

> But all things that are exposed are made
> manifest by the light, for whatever makes
> manifest is light.
>
> Ephesians 5:13 (NKJV)

The people who sat in darkness have seen a great light, and upon those who sat in the region and shadow of death Light has dawned.

Matthew 4:16 (NKJV)

For you were once darkness but now you are light in the Lord. Walk as children of light.

Ephesians 5:8 (NKJV)

Let your light so shine before men, that they may see your good works and glorify your Father in heaven.

Matthew 5:16 (NKJV)

You've probably cranked the handle on that box so many times you have carpal tunnel syndrome. The shape of the handle has worn callous into your palm in a cruel but comforting reminder that you've adapted dysfunction into normalcy. You don't quite know how to function without that jack-in-the-box until the hand of love covers yours and stills that ever-churning cycle of self-loathing and punishment.

I am not saying anything is easy, but with God, all things are possible. You may want to return to that jack-in-the-box out of habit, but habits can be broken. Light will gently permeate your soul if you let it until you can't help but shine effervescently. You become incandescent, and what love has already seen in you is now known by you.

Box of Bones

Let me begin by saying, I do not, nor will I ever have an actual box filled with bones in my closet, not even a thanksgiving wishbone, snapped in a friendly competition between myself and my sisters. I am not a taxidermist either. I do have things buried that like to rattle me from time to time, never letting old things die. There are also things in my life that have died and are nothing more than dry, brittle bones of buried dreams that I've lost heart to believe could ever be imbued with life again.

These rattling bones have followed me to our new home, tapping their ancient, gnarled, greedy phalanges on my shoulder, tempting me not to be present in the moment before me. The dry, lifeless bones mock me in their silence, reminding me of what once was or could have been, before collapsing into a catacomb of painful memories.

So much has happened since moving back to Georgia. We've been house-hunting nonstop. We found one we liked, several really, but we needed our house back in New Mexico to sell first. Houses are selling so quickly here, a fact I attribute to being PCS season for military families; moving time. Out with the old and in with the new. My husband and I have vastly different preferences for what we want in a home, resulting in minimal selections that meet both of our criteria. But we found a home that had it all: A pool, 1.5 acres, screened-in sunroom, a huge front porch, magnolia trees, gardenias, a workshop, and a shed. The inside of the home, however, needed some help. Okay, a lot of help. Granted, this was only the second house we'd seen, but we were ecstatic. I was ready to have friends over to sit on our porch swing and in the double seater rocking chair, sipping on coffee while the kids played joyfully with our new neighbors' children on their four-wheelers. Even our dogs are best friends.

We made an offer on the house. The kids, my husband, and I all prayed in agreement that the house was ours. We made plans to remodel and decorate. I went nuts on Pinterest too. When we got the news that we lost the bid to another buyer, our boys were devastated. Boy, oh boy, did they cry. They didn't want to hope or pray again for another home. Case in point, we can pray our will and be disappointed because it wasn't God's will. Back to the drawing board. More and more houses to see while the available homes began dwindling. We went to one after another, and another, and another. Throughout this entire process, my husband's new job weighing heavily on him. He wasn't receiving one-on-one training. Our kids had no one to play with, and they have been arguing, wrestling, and disrespecting each other and us nonstop.

Our female golden retriever attacked our papillon for the third time, the second horrible time though. That's right; she tried to eat him like a crunchy little snack. We have no idea why. He had bite marks on his face between his eyes, the back of his left ear, chest, throat, and shoulder. I'll spare you the gory details of the rest of his ripped skin. It was bad. Very bad. The emergency vet visit was $1,400. Since then, we've spent another $700, and I have had to call rescues and vets in case we had to have our golden put down; such horrible decisions. We moved our golden into her kennel and kept our papillon separate from her.

During this time, I had the worst sore throat and ear pain. Visions of years of recurring strep throat plagued my mind, plus the flu and possibly covid-19. My hubby took me to urgent care to be checked out, but he wasn't allowed inside. I went in alone, face mask in place. The bones in my face ached so badly, and vertigo had set in, my ears were burning internally, I had hot flashes, chills, lightheadedness, and more. Strep tests are bad enough. The flu tests are worse, but the covid-19 test: that *hurt*! I was begging the attendant to stop the test. He shoves a springy, too long swab up your nose and almost down your throat repeatedly, and it burns. You feel like you're choking, and your eyes tear up tremendously as you reach for the person's hand in an attempt to remove the invasive swab by force.

All drama aside, I was negative for strep, flu, and covid-19. It turned out to be a nasty sinus infection with postnasal drip. Thank God for antibiotics and pain medicine! My husband and I had a massive blowout of an argument on a walk. First time I've cried like that in a while. To top it off, a wonderful lady from my Bible study group died from cancer. She held my hand during our studies when I was depressed and attacked by suicidal thoughts.

A few days later, I said goodbye to my golden retriever as I handed her over to a wonderful woman from a rescue for golden retrievers. I drove away feeling like such a traitor to my girl. I've had nightmares each night and then dreams that have me in tears. Panic attacks have increased too. I turned introspective and blind to anyone or anything outside of my own circumstances. But, God. He got my attention with a daily devotional about the book of Ezekiel and the valley of dry bones being resurrected followed by a sermon by Steven Furtick on the same subject.

If that wasn't enough to get my attention, reading in the book of Ezekiel while listening to the sermon clenched the message God was sending. God was not only leading me to resurrect my lost hopes and dreams but to lay to rest some dead, dry bones from long ago that had drudged up memories of their existence quite unexpectedly.

All of this mess was just one hit after another, and then God opened my eyes to bigger problems. Bear with me now. When we moved here from New Mexico, I instantly noticed a shift in demographics. More people didn't look like me here, and I'm ashamed to say that discomfort overtook me I suddenly felt like the odd man out.

Memories flooded me of how I was raised not to be racist at all. I didn't care about the color of someone's skin, age, gender, money, faith, or lack thereof. These differences didn't faze me at all. My parents raised me to love. The structure they built in me was solid and true, but that wasn't to say there weren't opposing forces trying to rip apart what they taught me and bury those bones while replacing them with a box of bones of their own. These are the kind of bones passed down from generation to generation, hidden well within their family closet but rearing their ugly heads more and more voraciously and boldly as time goes on.

My best friend next door was amazing! We played together any chance we could get, her brothers were like brothers to me, her mom introduced me to bologna, cheese, and mustard sandwiches. I loved her mom! My friend and I played dress up and even had baths together when we were really young. We used wooden building blocks as pretend shaving razors for our legs. We spent the night at each other's homes and played catch out front with a football.

Neither one of us cared about the color of skin we had. We were just so happy to be friends! I cherish those years still, even though I haven't seen her in twenty-seven years. This, this right here, is what I want for our sons. I want them to love people, no matter what they look like or where they come from. I also want our sons to be loved by others, regardless of their skin color and where they've come from. These bones, this life in these bones, that's what I want holding our children up. It comes down to love.

As the enemy would have it, the ugly box of bones in the closet also vied for my attention. I distinctly remember a family friend's son having a rebel flag hanging in his room and exposing me to the use of the N-word at a very young age. On the way home from school one day, he was yelling it out at the top of his lungs from the bed of the truck towards unsuspecting students at a local high school. I did too. I had no idea what I was saying, but he sure did. Living in the south, I was exposed repeatedly to these kinds of racial slurs.

I didn't realize the seed these despicable bones would plant in my mind and how they'd battle the goodness that love had sown, a sickening plan of destruction, Satan has tricks. He sure does. Because this mess still rages on today with devastating effects. I see it everywhere. This box of bones wants to claw their way to life in the world and keep the enemy's plan for us to self-destruct, alive and well.

Don't you see it? People are killing each other over race, looting stores, rioting, slandering, and more. And guess what? The church needs to wake the heck up to the schemes the enemy has been using to keep us asleep, angry, divided, victimized, depressed, and anxious, not bringing glory to God as the body of Christ, under one King. Can't you see it? We have been torn apart as the body of Christ, turned inward and fighting each other.

This is like a self-detonation causing spiritual shrapnel to lodge in our bodies, crippling the church and delighting these wicked bones sent to distract and destroy us. But God, yes, I can say that. But God. He died and paid for us, to redeem us and save the world through Christ in us. Instead of being the church like we should be, we've been profaning God's holy name, dishonoring Him, each other, and ourselves. Sunday has become, what is said by many people to be the most segregated day in the country.

I don't know about you, but it is time to recognize the real enemy, the devil, take responsibility for our actions, stand alongside each other, and have a mass burial for these bones and their boxes. God has a plan. He will heal the bride of Christ and awaken the dead, dry bones of His people through us by His Holy Spirit. No more being sidetracked. No more introspecting. No more woe is me. No more victim mentality. No more excuses. Time to speak in love and faith and prophesy over what was dead, that God is mending back together and bringing back to life.

No more staring at someone who doesn't look like you and shuddering at the nasty, hateful thoughts that crop up from someone's box of bones passed down to you. No more hiding from the name-calling and derogatory comments. Time to stand up together and prophecy to the dead, dry bones of our fallen brothers and sisters in Christ and raise the church back to life and help her to her feet, bearing the image of God to the world.

This next portion may be a bit long, but I pray for you to see the situation we are in, paralleled with God's people and how He wants our involvement in the healing of the body of Christ so that we can properly display His love and glory to the world. He has a plan, and we get to be a part of it! I pray the Holy Spirit shows you what He showed me.

Moreover the word of the Lord came to
me, saying: "Son of man, when the house

of Israel dwelt in their own land, they defiled it by their own ways and deeds; to Me their way was like the uncleanness of a woman in her customary impurity. Therefore I poured out My fury on them for the blood they had shed on the land, and for their idols with which they had defiled it. So I scattered them among the nations, and they were dispersed throughout the countries; I judged them according to their ways and their deeds. When they came to the nations, wherever they went, they profaned My holy name—when they said of them, 'These are the people of the Lord, and yet they have gone out of His land.' But I had concern for My holy name, which the house of Israel had profaned among the nations wherever they went. Therefore say to the house of Israel, 'Thus says the Lord God: "I do not do this for your sake, O house of Israel, but for My holy name's sake, which you have profaned among the nations wherever you went. And I will sanctify My great name, which has been profaned among the nations, which you have profaned in their midst; and the nations shall know that I am the Lord," says the Lord God, "when I am hallowed in you before their eyes. For I will take you from among the nations, gather you out of all countries, and bring you into your own land. Then I will sprinkle clean water on you, and you shall be clean; I will cleanse you from all your filthiness and from all your idols. I will give you a new heart and put a new spirit within you; I will take the heart of stone out of your flesh and give you a heart of flesh. I will put My Spirit within you and cause you to walk in My statutes, and you will keep My judgments and do them. Then you shall dwell in the land that I gave to your fathers; you shall be My people, and I will be your God. I will deliver you from all your uncleanness. I will call for the grain and multiply it, and bring no famine upon you. And I will multiply the fruit of your trees and the increase of your fields, so that you need never again bear the reproach of famine among the nations. Then you will remember your evil ways and your deeds that were not good; and you will loathe yourselves in your own sight, for your iniquities and your abominations. Not for your sake do I do this," says the Lord God, "let it be known to you. Be ashamed and confounded for your own ways, O house of Israel!" 'Thus says the Lord God: "On the day that I cleanse you from all your iniquities, I will also enable you to dwell in the cities, and the ruins shall be rebuilt. The desolate land shall be tilled instead of lying desolate in the sight of all who pass by. So they will say, 'This land that was desolate has become like the garden of Eden; and the wasted, desolate, and ruined cities are now fortified and inhabited.' Then the nations which are left all around you shall know that I, the Lord, have rebuilt the ruined places and planted what was desolate. I, the Lord, have spoken it, and I will do it." 'Thus says the Lord God: "I will also let the house of Israel inquire of Me to do this for them: I will increase their men like a flock. Like a flock offered as holy sacrifices, like the flock at Jerusalem on its ⌈feast days, so shall the ruined cities be filled with flocks of men. Then they shall know that I am the Lord."'"

The hand of the Lord came upon me and brought me out in the Spirit of the Lord, and set me down in the midst of the valley; and it was full of bones. Then He caused me to pass by them all around, and behold, there were very many in the open valley; and indeed they were very dry. And He said to me, "Son of man, can these bones live?" So I answered, "O Lord God, You know." Again He said to me, "Prophesy to these bones, and say to them, 'O dry bones, hear the word of the Lord! Thus says the Lord God to these bones: "Surely I will cause breath to enter into you, and you shall live. I will put sinews on you and bring flesh upon you, cover you with skin and put breath in you; and you shall live. Then you shall know that I am the Lord."''" So I prophesied as I was commanded; and as I prophesied, there was a noise, and suddenly a rattling; and the bones came together, bone to bone. Indeed, as I looked, the sinews and the flesh came upon them, and the skin covered them over; but there was no breath in them. Also He said to me, "Prophesy to the breath, prophesy, son of man, and say to the breath, 'Thus says the Lord God: "Come from the four winds, O breath, and breathe on these slain, that they may live."''" So I prophesied as He commanded me, and breath came into them, and they lived, and stood upon their feet, an exceedingly great army. Then He said to me, "Son of man, these bones are the whole house of Israel. They indeed say, 'Our bones are dry, our hope is lost, and we ourselves are cut off!' Therefore prophesy and say to them, 'Thus says the Lord God: "Behold, O My people, I will open your graves and cause you to come up from your graves, and bring you into the land of Israel. Then you shall know that I am the Lord, when I have opened your graves, O My people, and brought you up from your graves. I will put My Spirit in you, and you shall live, and I will place you in your own land. Then you shall know that I, the Lord, have spoken it and performed it," says the Lord.'" Again the word of the Lord came to me, saying, "As for you, son of man, take a stick for yourself and write on it: 'For Judah and for the children of Israel, his companions.' Then take another stick and write on it, 'For Joseph, the stick of Ephraim, and for all the house of Israel, his companions.' Then join them one to another for yourself into one stick, and they will become one in your hand. "And when the children of your people speak to you, saying, 'Will you not show us what you mean by these?'—say to them, 'Thus says the Lord God: "Surely I will take the stick of Joseph, which is in the hand of Ephraim, and the tribes of Israel, his companions; and I will join them with it, with the stick of Judah, and make them one stick, and they will be one in My hand."' And the sticks on which you write will be in your hand before their eyes. "Then say to them, 'Thus says the Lord God: "Surely I will take the children of Israel from among the nations, wherever they have gone, and will gather them from every side and bring them into their own land; and I will make them one nation in the land, on the mountains of Israel; and one king shall be king over them all; they shall no longer be two nations, nor shall they ever be divided into two kingdoms again. They shall not defile themselves

anymore with their idols, nor with their detestable things, nor with any of their transgressions; but I will deliver them from all their dwelling places in which they have sinned, and will cleanse them. Then they shall be My people, and I will be their God "David My servant shall be king over them, and they shall all have one shepherd; they shall also walk in My judgments and observe My statutes, and do them. Then they shall dwell in the land that I have given to Jacob My servant, where your fathers dwelt; and they shall dwell there, they, their children, and their children's children, forever; and My servant David shall be their prince forever. Moreover I will make a covenant of peace with them, and it shall be an everlasting covenant with them; I will establish them and multiply them, and I will set My sanctuary in their midst forevermore. My tabernacle also shall be with them; indeed I will be their God, and they shall be My people. The nations also will know that I, the Lord, sanctify Israel, when My sanctuary is in their midst forevermore.""''"
Ezekiel 36:16–3; 37:1–28 (NKJV)

Do you see this? Can you imagine it? I don't know if I can say it any better than Scripture already has. God is going to show the world who He is by uniting His church and sanctifying His name, even though, through our actions, we defiled it and buried the bones of the Church body in a box. He's had enough. These dry bones have been rattling long enough, waiting for their resurrection day when they can breathe life once again. God will breathe His life into our dead, tired, dry bones. Our bodies will join back together bone by bone, sinew by sinew, organ by organ, and flesh to flesh in covering.

The Lord will rebuild from the ground up, cell by cell, what was once desolate. His body of believers will become like the garden of Eden. We will know how our actions landed us in a ditch and God's kindness as He reconstructs us into something even better. Our box of bones will be alive and kicking because we will have been cleansed and given new hearts of flesh. We will be healed. The world will watch and scratch their heads in confusion as the old stanky dry bones the enemy wants alive are obliterated, and we, the body of Christ, are alive to God. They will know something is different. They will know us by our love for one another. And the best part is, they will know it was God who did it.

I am speaking to the box of dry bones that gains flesh without hope. You have the Spirit of God, His breath, living inside of you. Rise, join together bone to bone, flesh to flesh, and live! Fight for each other, children, and the army of the living God.

> And I will make them one nation in the land, on the mountains of Israel; and one king shall be king over them all; they shall no longer be two nations, nor shall they ever be divided into two kingdoms again.
> Ezekiel 37:22 (NKJV)

Dear Jesus,

This book has been a lifetime in the making. It feels like I'm saying goodbye to a friend and also a weight. Please, make it make sense to the readers. Thank you for staying by my side during the writing process and in this mess with me. I've been through so very much and am still going through it. Just hearing you speak and giving me aha moments has honestly kept me going on days when I just didn't think I could take anymore.

Please help me to take courage and run with it! I want to run with you every single day! I cannot do this without you! I am literally shaking as I finish these last words. Stay close to me, Jesus, and help the readers know that they are so loved and cherished and that finding you and loving you and submitting their lives to you is the greatest adventure they will have this side of eternity!

In your name, Jesus, Amen.
And Love, Andrea

P.S.

To anyone who picks up this book and reads it, bless you! And thank you! I can not tell you how much reading other people's stories helped me during this last year. I pray mine blesses you! The most important thing I can tell you is that you are LOVED. Jesus loves you. He died for you. You are precious to Him. You are not a mistake. You are made in His image. He wants to save you and walk daily with you. He will never leave you or abandon you. You are worthy of love. You are precious!

"And now abide faith, hope, love, these three; but the greatest of these is love" (1 Corinthians 13:13, NKJV).